The Essence of
Strategic Management

The Essence of Management Series

The Essence of Strategic Management

Cliff Bowman

Cranfield School of Management

Prentice Hall

New York   London   Toronto   Sydney   Tokyo   Singapore

First published 1990 by
Prentice Hall International (UK) Ltd
66 Wood Lane End, Hemel Hempstead
Hertfordshire HP2 4RG
A division of
Simon & Schuster International Group

© Prentice Hall International (UK) Ltd, 1990

Typeset in 10/12 pt Palatino
by Keyset Composition, Colchester

Printed and bound in Great Britain by
BPCC Wheatons Ltd, Exeter

Library of Congress Cataloging-in-Publication Data

Bowman, Cliff.
    The essence of strategic management / Cliff Bowman.
        p. cm. — (The Essence of management series)
    Includes bibliographical references and index.
    ISBN 0-13-284738-8
    1. Strategic planning.   I. Title.   II. Series.
HD30.28.B685   1990
658.4 012—dc20

British Library Cataloguing in Publication Data

Bowman, Cliff
    Essence of strategic management,
    1. Companies. Management. Long-range planning
    I. Title   II. Series
    658.4012

                                              90-45140
    ISBN 0-13-284738-8   CIP

---

2 3 4 5   94 93 92 91

Contents

Contents

Preface

As strategic management texts tend to be weighty tomes, I was
intrigued by the publisher's challenge to write a practical guide to the
subject in a concise format. In trying to meet these requirements I have
had to exclude much material that is normally included in the more
conventional texts. In making the difficult decisions about what to
include (and what could reasonably be left out) I have been guided by
the experiences that I and my colleagues at Cranfield School of
Management have had in working with managers. If concepts and
techniques have passed the tough scrutiny of practising managers
then they have been included here. The more theoretical, esoteric and
less essential matter has been excluded (although this is, of course, a
matter of opinion).

To avoid producing a rather fragmented digest of the subject I have
imposed a rigid framework on the material, which I nevertheless hope
the reader will find logical and realistic. There are two particularly
contentious aspects of the book. The first is the approach to competitive strategy. Here one cannot ignore the contributions of Michael
Porter. I have tried to present his views fairly, and concisely, reserving
some doubts and criticisms to the end of Chapter 3. The second
contentious area is the treatment of corporate strategy (as opposed to
business level strategy). Although most textbooks tend to roll these
together, I have separated them. The bulk of the book is concerned
with business level strategy. The last chapter is concerned with
corporate strategy. The case study has been included to help the reader
practise some of the techniques of strategic management.

Lastly, I would like to thank Christine Bowman for her help in editing the book.

Cliff Bowman
February 1990

1

What is strategic management?

How did your organization reach the situation it is in today? Why is it producing these particular products or services? How come you happen to be located here? Why are you serving only certain parts of the marketplace? How did you end up with this particular group of senior managers? Why are you organized in this particular way?

All these questions address different but interrelated aspects of your organization, and all these aspects come together to influence how effective the organization will be in achieving its objectives. Decisions about products, location, structure and senior management appointments are all major decisions. They invariably make an impact (for better or worse) on the organization's performance. How these major (or 'strategic') decisions are made and how they are implemented can be defined as the process of strategic management.

Think for a moment about some of these questions and try to apply them to your organization. How were these decisions made, and how were they implemented?

Making strategic decisions

Let us concentrate first on how the decisions were made. It could be that your organization used a system like corporate planning to make these important decisions. If so then the decisions will have been made only after a great deal of information-gathering, analysis and forecasting. The corporate planning process would probably have involved not just the senior management team but also a number of staff analysts who would have done much of the technical work to help the senior managers in their deliberations. The outcome of this process would have been a plan for the whole organization for, say, the next five years. It is likely that this plan would then have been broken down into detailed budgets and action plans to be implemented by middle and junior managers. Figure 1.1 shows the steps in a corporate planning process.

If this process sounds familiar then you are working for an organization that has successfully implanted corporate planning, and, we might assume, is reaping the rewards of this logical and structured approach to making strategy.

However, it may be that this orderly, rational system does not square with your understanding of how things are done in your organization. Maybe you are familiar with a less structured approach to making decisions, one that is more *ad hoc* and opportunistic than the corporate planning process. It could well be that decision making in your organization seems to be more to do with reacting to crises and disasters, where the organization lacks a consistent view about what it is trying to achieve.

Between the extremes of corporate planning, on the one hand, and completely *ad hoc*, reactive decision making on the other, there lies a range of strategic decision making styles. In some organizations these decisions are the responsibility of the chief executive, who consults no-one else and writes no plans but nevertheless has a clear vision about the organization's future (such as in an owner-managed firm, or see Illustration 1A). In other situations the top management set broad guidelines to the managers of business units/profit centres/departments allowing these lower levels a fair degree of discretion in decision making (such as in a university).

It must be realized from the outset that there is no one best way to manage the strategy of an organization. A reactive, flexible style may suit a small firm in a rapidly changing environment (like, for example, a fashion clothing retailer), whereas the British Airports Authority would need to take a long-term view and to plan accordingly. Some organizations need to plan many years ahead, usually because it takes them a long time to make changes (e.g. building another runway at Gatwick), whereas others cannot plan ahead more than a few months because they face a very unpredictable environment.

We must also consider the nature of the organization's work. Some organizations are engaged in complex tasks where a great deal of expertise is required at many levels of the hierarchy (e.g. Glaxo).

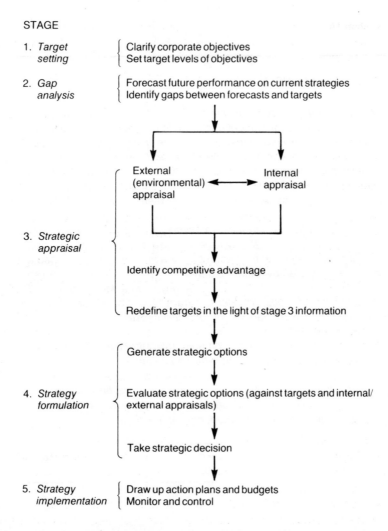

STAGE

1. *Target setting*
   - Clarify corporate objectives
   - Set target levels of objectives

2. *Gap analysis*
   - Forecast future performance on current strategies
   - Identify gaps between forecasts and targets

3. *Strategic appraisal*
   - External (environmental) appraisal ⟷ Internal appraisal
   - Identify competitive advantage
   - Redefine targets in the light of stage 3 information

4. *Strategy formulation*
   - Generate strategic options
   - Evaluate strategic options (against targets and internal/external appraisals)
   - Take strategic decision

5. *Strategy implementation*
   - Draw up action plans and budgets
   - Monitor and control

Figure 1.1 A corporate planning process in outline. (Adapted from J. Argenti, *Practical Corporate Planning* (London: Allen & Unwin, 1980).)

Others are highly diversified conglomerates where the head office could not always expect to be the best judge of the market situation facing a particular subsidiary (e.g. Unilever). In these circumstances it makes sense to decentralize many of the decisions that were considered above (e.g. what new products to develop, where to site a new plant). In these cases senior management at corporate HQ should

Illustration 1A

ROBERT MAXWELL

Maxwell operated from the ninth floor of the Mirror building. It was perfectly usual for three meetings to be in progress simultaneously. The dining room might hold a meeting with trade union officials; there could be an American print executive in his office, and a prospective recruit to his staff in the sitting room. Other people with appointments would be queuing up in the reception area while senior executives would be cajoling the appointments secretary to let them know when 'R.M.' would be free for 'just two minutes'.

The reason for the log jam was simply that delegation was virtually non-existent. Written authority for every new car and every new position on his papers, whether for a secretary or a managing director, had to be personally initialled by Maxwell. Senior executives had authority to spend up to set limits without reference, but they used it with care. Virtually all important negotiations, whether with trade unions or printers or computer manufacturers, were handled by Maxwell himself.

It is doubtful whether any other public company of comparable size in Britain was subject to quite such autocratic direction; certainly no other newspaper company operated in this manner (even Northcliffe listened to his brother Harold). With such centralization of control in the hands of this one man there were many delays and inefficiencies, last-minute switches of policy and ill-considered gestures. And yet, whatever the sceptics might say, the technique worked, most of the time.

Extracted from C. Wintour, 'The rise and fall of Fleet Street', *The Guardian*
(4 September 1989).

---

concern itself with setting broad guidelines which shape the decisions delegated to lower levels.

Figure 1.2 summarizes some of these points. The organization's actual situation (its 'realized strategy') can come about through the deliberate formulation and implementation of plans; or the realized strategy can emerge from a pattern in a stream of decisions ('emergent strategy'). Note that some attempts to plan strategy fail. Why this is so is explored in the next section.

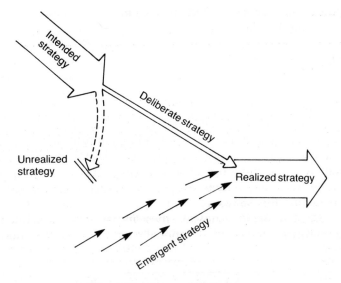

Figure 1.2 Forms of strategy.

Problems with corporate planning

It would be a mistake to assume that corporate planning has ever been strongly established in UK organizations. The technique was developed in the mid-1960s and based around ideas emerging from (largely US) business schools. The appeal of corporate planning lies in its apparently logical and analytical approach to the most important decisions that managers have to make. Some organizations have had good experiences using the technique, and even if the eventual plan does not get implemented, the process of drawing it up is usually beneficial.

Problems that crop up most frequently with corporate planning include the following:

1. Events overtake the plan.
2. The process stifles creativity and initiative.
3. There are unanticipated problems in implementing the plan.
4. Managers not involved in the planning process are not committed to the plan.

5. Short-term crises deflect management attention from implementing the plan.

This last point is probably the most significant reason that many 'good' plans are not implemented. Day-to-day operational problems soak up the scarcest resource in any organization: management time, talent, energy and commitment to change.

So far we have assumed that the plan is logical and rational. However, many planning groups tend to ignore in their deliberations the 'soft' issues in the organization. Such issues would include the formal and informal power relationships between people, their attitudes to change, their values and beliefs, the culture of the organization, the status relationships, and morale of the staff. A corporate plan that does not take these important aspects into account could hardly be described as 'rational', and yet many do ignore them.

Mission statements

'Mission statements' have become quite fashionable recently, and are seen by some managers as an alternative to corporate planning. Figure 1.3, from a leading US strategic management textbook, lists the establishing of a 'strategic mission' as the first phase in the strategic management process. The mission statement sets out the organization's ground rules to its approach to doing business, and good statements usually address the following:

1. The shared beliefs and values.

2. A definition of the business which covers the needs being satisfied, the chosen markets, how those markets will be reached, what technologies will be used in delivering the products/services.

3. It may also include the legitimate claims of relevant stakeholders (e.g. employees, shareholders, customers, society, the City).

4. Attitudes to growth and financing, decentralization, innovation, etc.

However, in order to answer some of these questions management may need to conduct a substantial amount of research and analysis.

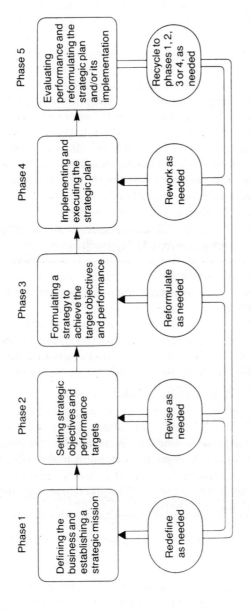

Figure 1.3 The strategic management process. (From A. Thompson and A. Strickland, *Strategic Management: Concepts and cases* (Business Publications, Inc., 1987).)

For example: What precisely are the needs being satisfied by our products/services? What markets should we be aiming at? What other technologies might we use? What are the shared values in this organization? Do we like them? The drawing up of a good mission statement would therefore require almost as much time and effort as the corporate planning process. This need not be a problem as long as management does not rush into defining the mission statement before these questions have been thoroughly aired. Referring to Figure 1.3, we would expect an organization embarking upon a more structured approach to strategic management to cycle between phases 1, 2 and 3 frequently until such time as the team felt comfortable with the emerging mission statement. In contrast, a well-established organization well versed in strategic thinking would be more likely to be revisiting phases 3, 4 and 5; only rarely would it be necessary to review the mission statement.

There is little doubt that a well-drawn-up mission statement is a valuable component in the effective strategic management of an organization. The question is whether it is the best place to start the strategy-making process. In this book I have taken the view that the easiest way into the strategic management process is through a structured analysis of the organization's industry environment. My reasons are as follows:

1. It eases the management team into the process of thinking strategically without them having immediately to confront vital and potentially controversial issues.

2. It introduces some structure into the team's thinking which invariably develops new insights into the industry that they thought they knew everything about. This then encourages broader thinking, and tends to increase the appetite for, and acceptance of, other strategic management tools and techniques.

We return to the mission statement in Chapter 6 to look at the role it can play in managing strategic changes.

Developing a strategic perspective

There are a variety of reasons why some organizations do not develop sound strategic management processes. Some of the most important are as follows:

1. There is a lack of awareness within the top management team of the organization's true situation. This could be due to poor information systems which are not providing the management with the information it needs to judge correctly the organization's position with respect to competitors, buyer trends, relative costs, etc.

2. The senior managers are collectively deluding themselves about the organization's position. This can come about, paradoxically, where the senior managers consider themselves to be a tightly knit group. They share the same stereotyped views of the competition, the customers and the workforce. They 'reinterpret' or ignore unpleasant information that does not fit in with their preferred way of looking at the world.

3. There are some powerful managers who have a vested interest in maintaining the status quo. Their position and status depend upon the perpetuation of the existing strategy and are likely to discourage people from asking challenging questions.

4. A common problem results from top management being too locked into everyday, operational problems. This gives the managers no time to consider longer-term issues, nor does it prepare them to take a strategic perspective on the organization.

5. Past success in the organization can make people blind to the current situation the organization faces. Moreover, past success encourages management to stick with tried and trusted strategies which may be inappropriate to present and future circumstances.

6. Changing direction can be seen as an admission that what was done before was a mistake. This makes managers who are closely identified with these past decisions reluctant to see the organization move off in a different direction.

7. One last reason for inertia results from a lack of awareness within senior management about quite why the organization is successful. If it is unable to pin down what it is that the firm does that gives it a competitive edge, then it is likely to 'leave well alone' for fear

that the goose that lays the golden egg may inadvertently be destroyed.

Ranged against these forces for preserving the status quo are a number of situations or actions that can help to raise the strategic awareness of the top management:

1. A serious downturn in performance can encourage the senior management group to begin reassessing the appropriateness of the current strategy.
2. A surprise move from a major competitor can act as a stimulus to the top management.
3. Scandals, and 'whistle blowing' from disaffected managers, staff or customers can provoke an urgent need to reappraise the organization's position.
4. A newcomer to the top management group can be the catalyst for strategic change.
5. A programme of management development, even if not directed at the top management team, can start people questioning the status quo.
6. The need to raise capital may require the preparation of a business plan to satisfy investors that the firm has a viable future strategy.
7. Takeover by another corporation that requires the submission of formal plans and budgets.

One rather depressing fact of business life is that in many organizations the tendency to leave things as they are is very strong. It can often require a state of near crisis to be reached before top management pays more than lip service to strategic management.

Perhaps the biggest obstacle to thinking about, developing and implementing new strategies is the need to run today's business. The day-to-day events drive out most strategic good intentions. The only way to make sure that this does not happen is to make the process of developing strategy a *formal* one. This does not mean having endless planning meetings, reams of paperwork and stifling procedures. At its most basic it simply means putting entries into diaries to the effect that one day we are all going to lift up our heads from the daily grind and consider the future of the organization. This meeting, and what you do to follow it up, can be as relaxed and informal as you like: the only requirement is that you make explicit the time taken out to look at strategy.

Organizations or firms?

The bulk of literature on strategic management is written with the reader from a private sector business organization in mind, making only passing reference to 'not-for-profit' (NFP) organizations (but see Bowman and Asch, 1987, for a discussion of strategic management in not-for-profits). This is acceptable only if you can assume that the tools and techniques of strategic management can be applied equally well to both types of organization.

I am increasingly of the view that many of the techniques of strategic management introduced in this book *can* be usefully applied to both NFPs and firms. However, there are differences between the two that are particularly relevant to strategic management. These differences flow from the fundamental purpose or purposes for which the two types of organization were established, in other words, from their objectives.

We shall take a very straightforward approach in our discussion of the objectives that firms pursue: we shall assume that firms need to make profits and that all other objectives (e.g. sales growth, market share, social responsibility, caring for employees) take a lower priority. That is not to say that these (and other) objectives are not important or relevant to many firms, merely that, when it comes to the crunch the firm that does not make a profit does not survive. We can view some of these other objectives more as ways of making profits rather than as objectives in their own right (e.g. trying to increase market share because it is linked to profitability). We also take a rather jaundiced view of various social objectives that are promoted by some managements for public relations reasons. For example, 'this firm cares about the environment' (as long as it does not cost anything).

In some firms other objectives not directly related to profits can, from time to time, predominate. For instance, survival may be of paramount importance to a firm in dire straits, but this must be a temporary objective. In other circumstances, notably where the shareholders are not in a position to influence directly the management of the firm, 'managerial' objectives may come to the fore (like empire building, enhancing status through company cars and other perks). These managerial objectives can persist, although there may come a point where profits fall so low that shareholders eventually reassert their power. Up until this point, of course, the firm must still be making some level of profit.

If you accept the notion that firms exist to make money, then

11

managing the firm's strategy becomes a much clearer task. Other ideas can be evaluated against the profit objective and performance can be measured and compared with that of other firms. Above all, the basic need to make profits can underpin the entire management process, enhancing the authority and the decision-making abilities of management. This clear goal can help guide decision-making at all levels of the firm, not just at the top.

Now consider the situation of the not-for-profit organization: for example, a comprehensive school. Education must be its objective, but how do we measure performance? Look at pass rates in GCSE examinations. This straightforward interpretation of the purpose of the school may suit some of those associated with the school, but others may see different aims as being important. For example, developing all the different talents of children (which would include music, dance, art, sport, drama, hobbies, etc). There is a strong lobby for religious education, while others complain about political indoctrination (there is either too much, or not enough). Most people would acknowledge the school's role in preparing children to take a useful role in society. This can extend to having a strong vocational orientation in the way that subjects are selected and taught. Others see this preparation for life to be more to do with developing the children's personality and social skills.

To complicate matters, who controls the school? We know that in the last resort shareholders have the power over the firm, but which group of 'stakeholders' prevails if there are conflicting objectives in the school? Is it the teachers, the parents, the local authority, the Department of Education, or the pupils? The confusion about who controls the school, coupled with the lack of clarity (and measurability) of objectives, makes the strategic management task extremely difficult. The absence of a 'bottom line' (like profits) means that the management of the school cannot act with clarity and certainty in making decisions. Good strategic managers in these circumstances tend to be able to combine acute political and interpersonal skills (to manage the disparate interest groups) with a clear set of values, or a 'vision'. Armed with this clarity of purpose they are then able to set direction and make judgements between conflicting requirements. So in this sense, the strategic managers of NFPs are more in need of well-developed 'strategies' or 'missions' (if they are going to inspire others, give them a sense of direction and a feeling of confidence) than managers in firms.

Corporate versus business level strategy making

There is an important distinction to be made between strategy making at the corporate level and strategy making at the level of the individual business unit. For the purposes of this book, a business unit is defined as a self-contained organization that is serving a particular market with a limited range of related products or services. The performance of the business unit would usually be measured by its profitability. Thus, an independent firm (i.e. one not controlled by a parent company) would be a business unit, as would a division of a large corporation if it met the criteria set out above. So a diversified conglomerate (like Hanson) would be made up of a large number of business units.

Chapters 2 to 6 concentrate on strategic management at the business unit level. All the techniques and examples introduced are appropriate to business units. Chapter 2 looks outside the business unit and introduces some techniques for analyzing the industry and the competition. Chapter 3 presents the latest thinking on competitive strategy, and Chapter 4 follows through the organizational implications of pursuing different competitive strategies. Chapter 5 looks inside the business at the organizational realities. This then prepares us for the problems of managing strategic change, which are covered in Chapter 6. The structure of the book is summarized in Figure 1.4.

Chapter 7 is devoted to strategy-making at the corporate level. We have made this distinction because the strategic issues are sufficiently different at the two levels that to deal with them simultaneously invites confusion.

Developing skills in strategic management

You cannot learn to drive a car by reading a book about it. In the same way, if you want to develop your strategic management skills you need to practise. Rather than experimenting directly on your organization the case study below can be used to try out some of the ideas and techniques that are introduced in the book. Read through the case a couple of times to familiarise yourself with the firm. The tasks at the end of the following chapters refer back to it.

At the end of the book there is a case study appendix containing the distilled wisdom of hundreds of managers who have tackled the

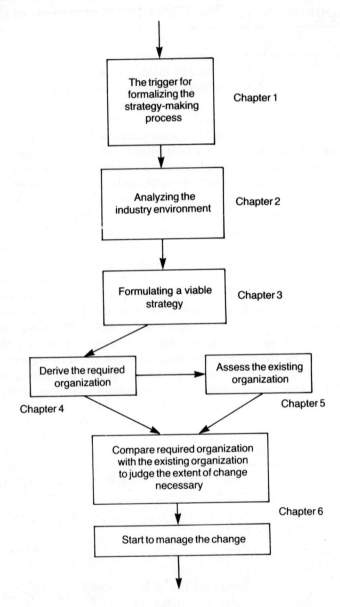

Figure 1.4 Outline of the book.

Workgear case study. After tackling the tasks you may like to compare
your views with theirs.

Case study: Workgear Ltd

Les Barnes, the managing director, was worried. At the age of 62, after
a long career in the textile industry, at a time when he had thought life
would be easier, he seemed to be faced with more problems than ever.
Previously in facing the vagaries of the market, he had been able to take
for granted the unity of the company, now he doubted the firm itself –
the people who made it up and their ability to work together.

History

The company had begun in 1927 as S. Ramsey & Co. Samuel Ramsey,
working in Bradford, purchased a site in the town from which to
operate a textile business with his son. After initial prosperity and
wartime production for the services, the business faltered and by 1967
the father's old age, together with the son's lack of interest, resulted in
a change of ownership and control. The run-down company, its
fixtures, fittings and machinery were bought out by a group comprising the general manager, Les Barnes, an executive director Alan
Chadwick, and two of Chadwick's (a qualified accountant) clients – a
local grocer and the owner of a company engaged in producing
ventilation equipment. With equal shareholdings, the four became
directors of the company. In effect the interest of the two outsiders
remained purely financial. Alan Chadwick became financial director
and chairman and Les Barnes, managing director. An outside appointment was made to fill the post of general manager, but after a short
while he left, as did his successor.

In terms of both machinery and sales, the company has been allowed
to run down. Working within the existing building, which the younger
Ramsey continued to own and rent to the company on a lease
renewable every seven years, Les Barnes and Alan Chadwick set to the
task of earning a return on their investment and paying back the
additional bank borrowings they had been forced to make.

In 1967 the business had 70 employees and produced an average of
1,200 garments per week. Over the following twenty years, employ-

ment rose to the present level, 127, with output at an average of 6,000 garments per week.

In 1982 the company changed its name to Workgear Ltd and revised its organization to the present form (Appendix 1). A designer, Colin Kelly, and a new factory manager, Arthur Fuller, were appointed and the existing factory manager, Stan Lewis, promoted to general manager. A cutting room manager, a work study engineer and the vacant post of a specialist in marketing were also appointed. At present, Workgear have three sales representatives, one in Somerset (for the south-west and parts of Wales), one in London (for London and the south-east and major customers) and the sales executive, based at the factory. The marketing post, held by Keith Williams, is not related to the day-to-day control of the sales force but exists to examine the potential of markets available to Workgear and to maintain contact with the big buyers. (It was on Williams's advice that the firm first entered the linen hire market.) At present, he is assessing the potential for export sales to Europe.

Products and markets

Since its foundation, in 1927, the company has produced and sold only industrial clothing (workwear – overalls, boilersuits, jackets, trousers and skirts). These are increasingly being worn by employees not only in manufacturing industries but also in the retail trades (e.g. supermarket staff) and the transport industry, by a range of personnel from van drivers to managers.

Keith Williams believes that the use of 'appropriate clothing' in implementing health and safety legislation, and the increasing self-awareness of company image will result in a growing demand for Workgear's products.

The sales are to two main types, to linen hire companies (industrial laundries who hire out the garments to the final user) and to the final user (see Figure 1). At present the company's sales are 50/50 (linen hire/final user). Among the final user customers are Boots, Kodak, Ross Foods, Metal Box, Sunblest, Danish Bacon Company and a number of supermarkets. The linen hire companies (including such companies as Advanced Linen and Initial Services, many of which belong to larger, non-laundry groups) provide final users with the required garments on a hire basis (as low as £1.50 per employee per week) and launder the garments for the hirer.

Workgear's product differs between the two types of customer. The

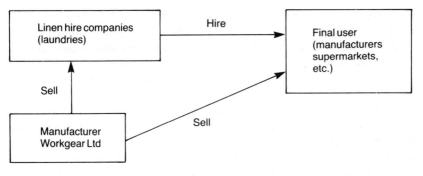

Figure 1

garments sold to hire companies tend to be bulk sales, allowing long runs (hundreds of garments) in one colour, size and design: a production which is much easier to schedule (Appendix 2) than the sales to final users (tens of garments). Sales to the laundries keep the firm busy, but Stan Lewis sees final user sales as the money-makers.

Whilst both types of sale involve negotiating with a specific person, an industrial buyer, the sales are distinct in the influences which are exerted upon the design specification. Final user firms are more willing to listen to the advice of Workgear's designer. Designs for linen hire companies begin with a basic design by Workgear, which is subjected to evaluation and comments by the company that will hire the garment. The opinions of all parties (accountants, safety officers, trade unions and the employees) are collated to a specification which is enforced upon the supplying company. Whilst the process may claim to be democratic its products are seldom aesthetic or cost-effective.

The material for both types of customer is the same, a top-quality fabric containing man-made fibres, bought from Klopman's, an Italian subsidiary of Du Pont's. The fabric's quality is known and fully accepted by the hire companies. With a three-year garment life and baked-in creases, the finished product is strong and smart, requiring a minimum of pressing during its cleaning.

The quality of the fabric is matched by the precision of the garment. The degree of precision which is required is far greater than that which would be required in a retail garment. Recently a linen hire buyer rejected a sample with a pocket ½ cm away from his specification.

The appointment of a designer to discuss with the customer his requirements and ideas has resulted in the ability to produce an individualistic product for each customer.

Although the quality and service provided by Workgear is appreciated by buyers, the gaining of contracts for bulk orders has become fiercely competitive. Until a few years ago, Workgear was able to follow a general pricing policy of full product cost plus ten per cent. Now the most important factor in deciding which company gains the contract is competitive price. Knowledgeable customers (thoroughly informed as to the costs of material, labour and production times) are able to assess Workgear's cost of production. This and the fiercely competitive bidding for contracts have increasingly depressed margins, due to the prices being negotiated being based on marginal costs.

The most recent linen hire contract for which the company quoted attracted fifteen other bids. The buyer took the best six quotations and divided the order among them at the price given in the lowest quotation. In view of the extreme competition for linen hire sales, and the consequent depression of margins, Workgear has recently sought to increase the proportion of their sales to final users.

Production

Stan Lewis (the general manager) and George Webb (the executive engineer) came to see increased efficiency as a route to the company's survival – allowing the firm to operate inside the market price. They backed this belief by spending £500,000 on efficiency (work study, machine modifications, new machines, and the operation of incentive schemes) during the past twelve months. Although nobody specializes in cost control, management refer to standards (established by the work study consultants) and calculate variances on production.

In retrospect, Stan Lewis sees the spending on efficiency as part of a continuing Workgear strategy. George Webb, who left last month after an argument with the managing director, had been with Ramsey's for thirty years. With a unique sense of the building's space limitations and the demands of the productive process, he had over the past fifteen years conducted a continuing and successful campaign of machine modification, new machine evaluation, troubleshooting, removal of inhibiting walls and fixtures and even the design of measuring devices to speed final garment inspection (see Appendix 2 for additional information).

Stan Lewis believes the absolute limit upon production capacity (a limit set by the building's size) would, even with more machinery, be 9,000 garments per week. The company has recently reached a rate of 7,000 garments per week.

New machinery and work study schemes have stretched the management to the limit. As a consequence of the present burden on management, Stan Lewis has shelved the recurring question of Workgear moving to a larger site, away from the physical constraints of their present rented building, to one of the many available locations in the town.

Management and personnel

Stan Lewis sees his major task as that of co-ordinator and resolver of the clashes that occur within the management team. He believes that the management group of ten men is too small to be able to allow continued divisions.

Training is not seen, by any of the executives, as an area of major concern. None of the managers has received anything beyond a technical training. Such management training as has taken place has involved sporadic attendance on short courses, normally those for which the training board pays a substantial grant. The training of operatives is informal, on the job, and completed within six weeks.

Turnover among the operatives is very low (such turnover as occurs is mostly due to marriage, pregnancy and moving from the area). Good wages and a friendly atmosphere with employees known and treated as individuals has resulted in many of the women being with the firm for a long time.

Stan Lewis, as general manager, feels he is responsible for the recruitment and supervision of the firm's management. He himself is discontented and is considering leaving the company. As a young man his five years of experience as general manager have left him little to learn from the company and he considers that the only real improvement in his position would be a place on the board. Recently a friend of Stan's has set up in his own business. With a bank loan of £2,000 using outworkers, he has celebrated a highly profitable first year of sales to the retail trade.

Recent performance

Despite the problems, Stan is able to look with a degree of satisfaction at the company's recent sales performance. From a situation, only a few years ago, when 5–6 weeks of orders was considered good, Workgear is now operating a 32-week delivery, despite its increased capacity. A lot of business has followed contract bidding. Some has arisen from customers recommending the firm to others; indeed, the company's name is probably as important as its advertising. In an industry that does not use mail shots, Workgear's advertising has been restricted to competition by the occasional advertisement in the trade papers. However, a brochure was produced (for a European exhibition) in conjunction with Klopman's, the cloth suppliers, who shared the printing costs. Despite this effort, exports have been negligible.

The forecasting of sales tends to be an exercise shared by management, with some assistance from the company's bank. Essentially the process consists of taking the previous year's sales figures and stating reasons for adding to or subtracting from this figure. (Fortunately the larger buyers give suppliers an indication of their likely requirements for the coming year, whereas the smaller buyers and final users are often a surprise factor.) Because the forecasting exercise is always conservative, a persistent tendency is to exceed the sales forecast, bringing an unexpected profit bonus. This gain has been complemented recently by increases in efficiency.

The future

Recent meetings have unearthed the following views on the future.

Among several large contracts imminent for tender is British Airports Authority. The BAA order would be for a great range of outwear including that for reception staff, waitresses, etc. – garments that are considered to be up-market – involving individualistic design, decoration and the highest quality. It will be 'piloted' at Heathrow. The BAA tender would be a final user sale. The buyers would be far less experienced than those of a linen hire company. However, they would appreciate aspects of quality-service, design and a prompt delivery related to their own phased introduction of the garments. A range of sizes and fits to allow for the requirements of particular employees would be necessary. Stan Lewis considers Workgear's design experience and quality production are well suited to such requirements.

Supermarket sales place an emphasis upon prompt delivery, and are usually quite profitable.

Unlike linen hire sales, initial sales to final users usually result in follow-on orders, provided the price quoted for those orders remains reasonable. Yet while attractive, such sales are also a daunting prospect. The choice of fabrics, the estimation of replacement needs for use-damaged garments, the time-consuming problems of specification would all be left to Workgear to decide. They are viewed as the experts by the new customer. Failure would prove costly, both in profit from that sale and loss of reputation and future orders.

Selling through retailers to consumers holds few attractions for any of the executives. An emphasis on cheapness rather than quality, the tendency towards shorter production runs, and more extensive advertising, together with the necessity of employing more sales representatives, are all taken as good reasons for not entering this market.

A further point for discussion is changes in the linen hire industry, an increasing trend among final users to buy their own on-premises laundry (OPL) facilities, purchase their own stocks of garments and enjoy consequent savings on the cost of the hire service. The producers of laundry facilities are currently putting increased effort into encouraging the use of their machines in OPL. Three years ago Kodak bought a laundry facility for £250,000, an investment which paid for itself after eighteen months.

The contrary view publicizes the problems of water, effluent, staff and legal issues. Nevertheless, a competitor of approximately the same size has begun a joint venture with a machine manufacturer to sell OPL facilities and garments as a 'package'.

Lantex, a growing group of companies producing workwear, children's wear and umbrellas, recently offered to acquire Workgear. The offer was declined by the board after consultation with the auditors.

Whilst the senior executives of Workgear are keenly interested in the implications of these changes for the firm's future direction, they realize that their influence upon such decisions is minimal. These decisions are taken solely by the managing director. At the best, slight attention is paid to the advice of the senior executives. While the situation is both confusing and upsetting to the executives, it appears to gain the tacit approval of the other three shareholders and of the bank. The dividend decision is shared between Alan Chadwick and Les Barnes.

A number of incidents has recently led to a widening of the gulf between the senior executives and Barnes. Six months ago, during the installation of a work study scheme, Stan Lewis built up the stock of work in progress to allow for the fall in production rate during changeover to the new scheme. Barnes found out about the increased stocks and insisted on their reduction in order to regain a normal stock ratio. There followed a period of several weeks in which the machinists had insufficient work and were paid an allowance for waiting time.

21

Another unpopular decision was the filling of a vacancy for a sales representative without the sales executive (Larry Ames) being consulted.

Note

This case has been adapted from 'S. Ramsey & Co. Ltd' by Dr D. Jennings of Trent Polytechnic by M. D. Scott of Cranfield School of Management as a basis for class discussion.

Appendix 1 Workgear Ltd organization chart

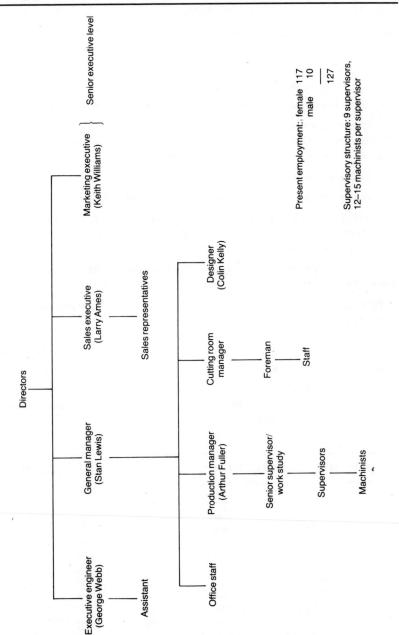

Directors

Senior executive level

Executive engineer (George Webb)

General manager (Stan Lewis)

Sales executive (Larry Ames)

Marketing executive (Keith Williams)

Assistant

Office staff

Sales representatives

Production manager (Arthur Fuller)

Cutting room manager

Designer (Colin Kelly)

Senior supervisor/ work study

Foreman

Supervisors

Staff

Machinists

Present employment: female 117
male   10
                    ———
                    127

Supervisory structure: 9 supervisors,
12–15 machinists per supervisor

Appendix 2 Production Flow

Store→issuing of fabric→mark–cutout→divide parts to workable sets of garments→machining, buttonholes, pocket reinforcing, etc.→final quality control→press→fold→package

Length of process: average (cut to out) 6 weeks.

Number of operators involved: average garment 13.

At present pressing is a bottleneck: lack of space for more presses; existing presses worked 11 hours per day for 4 days and 8 hours for 1 day.

The cutting room is also at capacity working.

Generally the factory works a single-shift five-day week plus overtime.

An activity sample, by the work study engineer, established that 75 per cent of certain operator time involved measuring the garment prior to a machine operation by that operator.

Also, some operators were spending 40–50 per cent of their time on jobs which were not part of their specific job description.

Scheduling is based upon the cutting room. Orders are attended to by priority (customer size, age of order, etc.). Within this the sequence of cutting is determined by the production manager (Arthur Fuller) attempting to ensure a mixture of operations that will not leave his machines unevenly loaded.

Stocks held include: cutting room, a minimum of 3,000 garments.
machine room, up to four weeks' work in progress.

Appendix 3 Percentage breakdown of turnover

	Linen hire	Supermarkets	Other final users
1986/7	50	10	40
1985/6	85	5	10
1984/5	62	20	18
1983/4	43	13	44
1982/3	0	15	85

Appendix 4 Annual turnover

	£m
1987/8	17.5 (estimate)
1986/7	15.0
1985/6	11.2
1984/5	8.4
1983/4	6.3
1982/3	5.0

Appendix 5 Annual income statements 1983–7

		£000						
		1983/4		1984/5		1985/6		1986/7
Turnover		6,260		8,380		11,200		15,020
Cost of goods, sold at standard cost								
Materials	3,330		4,780		6,830		9,740	
Labour	1,050		1,450		1,900		2,400	
Factory overhead	1,070	5,450	1,200	7,430	1,480	10,210	1,780	13,920
Variance adjustments								
Materials	(60)		(120)		(200)		(250)	
Labour	50		30		100		200	
Factory overhead	100	90	60	(30)	150	50	200	150
Actual cost of goods sold		5,360		7,460		10,160		13,770
Other expenses								
Admin. salaries	160		180		200		210	
Sales and marketing	160		180		210		230	
Directors' salaries	270		280		340		420	
Interest	20	610	20	660	60	810	180	1,040
Total costs		5,970		8,120		10,970		14,810
Net profit before tax		290		260		230		210
Tax		141		126		105		71
Net profit after tax		149		134		125		139
Dividends		80		80		80		80
Retained		£69		£54		£45		£59

Appendix 6 Annual balance sheets 1983–7

	1983/4 £	1984/5 £	1985/6 £	1986/7 £
Fixed assets				
Land and buildings	200,000	200,000	200,000	200,000
Plant and equipment	597,400	556,400	551,000	978,000
Motor vehicles	200,550	180,200	179,500	192,500
Office equipment	81,050	78,000	80,000	75,000
Total fixed assets	1,079,000	1,014,600	1,010,500	1,445,500
Current assets				
Stock	498,200	734,600	1,127,000	1,757,850
Debtors	250,800	356,300	497,200	698,000
Cash	7,200	3,900	2,500	2,000
	756,200	1,094,800	1,626,700	2,457,850
Current liabilities				
Creditors	202,300	341,300	464,400	857,600
Bank overdraft	131,000	166,700	255,800	597,400
Taxation	276,900	322,400	263,000	265,000
Dividends	80,000	80,000	80,000	80,000
	690,200	910,400	1,063,200	1,800,000
Working capital	66,000	184,400	563,500	657,850
Net capital employed	1,145,000	1,199,000	1,574,000	2,103,350
Financed by:				
Share capital	800,000	800,000	800,000	800,000
Retained earnings	345,000	399,000	474,000	503,350
Bank loan			200,000	200,000
Hire purchase commitments			100,000	600,000
Net capital employed	1,145,000	1,199,000	1,574,000	2,103,350

2

Analyzing the environment

Let us begin our analysis of the firm's situation by taking a structured look at its industry environment. We shall assume, at this stage, that by 'industry' we mean the firms that compete directly with each other in serving a distinct market with similar products or services. We use Porter's Five Forces model to gain insights into the competitiveness of the firm's industry. Later in the chapter we look at the wider macro-environment.

The Five Forces model

Figure 2.1 depicts the five forces that determine the extent of competition in an industry. The rationale behind this model is that industry profitability is not determined by what the product looks like, nor whether it embodies high or low technology: it is determined by the structure of the industry.

Competitive rivalry

This is the most obvious form of competition: the head-to-head rivalry between firms making similar products and selling them in the same market. Rivalry can be intense and cut-throat, or it may be governed by unwritten 'rules': gentlemen's agreements which help the industry to avoid the damage that excessive price-cutting, advertising and promotion expenses can inflict on profits. Competition can be restricted to

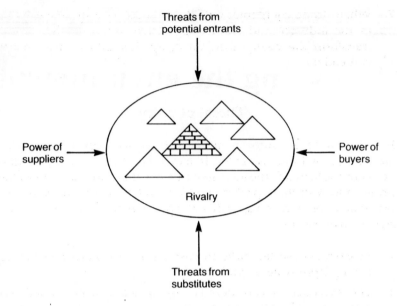

Figure 2.1   The Five Forces model of competition.

one dimension (e.g. price) or many (e.g. service, product quality, retail outlets, advertising, product innovation, credit).

Rivalry is usually intense where some of the following conditions are in evidence:

1. As the number of competitors increases and as they become more equal in size and capability.
2. When demand for the product is growing slowly.
3. When competitors are tempted by industry conditions to use price cuts or other competitive weapons to boost unit volume.
4. When competitors' products and services are so similar that customers incur low costs in switching from one brand to another.
5. When it costs more to get out of a business than to stay in and compete.
6. Rivalry becomes more volatile and unpredictable the more diverse competitors are in terms of their strategy, personalities, corporate priorities, resources and countries of origin.

7. When strong companies outside the industry acquire weak firms in the industry and launch aggressive, well-funded moves to transform the newly acquired competitor into a major market contender.

Threat of entry

If it is easy to get into an industry then, as soon as profits look attractive, new firms will enter. If demand for the industry's products does not rise to match the increased capacity that entry has caused then prices, and with them profits, are likely to fall. So the threat of entry places an upper limit on an industry's profitability. The most common *barriers* to entry are:

1. Economies of scale. These are cost advantages that accrue through having large-scale operations.
2. The existence of considerable cost benefits to be gained from experience. Here the advantages stem not from large-scale facilities but from the experience gained through repeatedly producing the product or service many times.
3. Brand preferences and customer loyalty making it difficult for a new entrant to prise customers away from their existing suppliers.
4. Capital requirements. Just the sheer up-front costs of entering the industry act as a deterrent (e.g. aerospace, oil refining).
5. Cost disadvantages independent of size. These might be due, for example, to access to cheaper labour or raw materials.
6. Access to distribution channels. If you cannot reach the customer as effectively as the incumbent firms then it will not be your products or services that are sold.
7. Government actions and policies: legislation, tariff and non-tariff barriers, patents, etc.

Threat of substitutes

For our purposes a substitute is something that meets the same needs as the product produced in the industry. If the substitute becomes more attractive in terms of price, performance or both, then some buyers will be tempted to move their custom away from the firms in the industry. If substitutes pose a credible threat, then, firms in the industry will be prevented from raising their prices or from failing to develop and improve their products/services.

When we think of substitutes we must start really to understand the needs that our industry is satisfying. For example, why do people buy a watch? Obviously, to tell the time, but is that the only need that is being met? Watches that simply tell the time can be bought for a few pounds so why spend thousands? Clearly the watch is meeting other needs like status and fashion; they are also bought as presents. This then raises the question of what substitutes might meet these needs? Status can be expressed through other purchases, e.g. cars, clothes, holidays. So when we look for where threats from substitutes might come from we need to cast our net quite wide, and unless sellers can upgrade quality or reduce prices via cost reduction they may risk low growth in sales and profits because of the in-roads that substitutes may make.

The competition from substitutes is affected by the ease with which buyers can switch to a substitute. A key consideration is usually the buyer's switching costs (the costs facing the buyer in changing from one product to a substitute product). For example, if an airline has an all-Boeing fleet, then the switching costs of moving to a mixed Boeing/Airbus fleet would include flight crew training, maintenance training and spares.

Power of buyers

Powerful buyers can bargain away potential profits from the firms in the industry. They can cause firms to undercut each other in order to get the buyer's business, and they can use their power to extract other benefits from firms like quality improvements, credit, etc.

Buyers are powerful in the following situations:

1. When customers are few in number and they purchase in large quantities.
2. When customers' purchases represent a sizeable percentage of the selling industry's total sales.
3. When the selling industry comprises large numbers of small sellers.
4. When the item being purchased is sufficiently standardized that customers can both find other suppliers easily and switch to them at virtually zero cost.

5. When the item being bought is not an important input.
6. When it is economically feasible for customers to purchase the input from several suppliers rather than one.

Power of suppliers

In a similar vein to buyers, suppliers of vital resources to the industry can exact high prices, leading to a squeeze on profits through higher input costs. Such suppliers would include suppliers of raw materials, power, skilled labour, components, etc.

Suppliers are powerful where:

1. The input is, in one way or another, important to the buyer.
2. The supplier industry is dominated by a few large producers who enjoy reasonably secure market positions and who are not beleaguered by intensely competitive market conditions.
3. Suppliers' respective products are unique to the extent that it is difficult or costly for buyers to switch from one supplier to another.

The concept of supplier can be extended to include the supply of management expertise, skilled labour and the supply of capital. Clearly, these vital resources are rarely in abundance, and firms are often required to minimize their dependence on outside sources of supply through developing their own managers, training their staff and by financing expansion through retained earnings.

The overall attractiveness of the industry

If all the five forces are strong industry profitability would be expected to be low regardless of the products/services being produced. Conversely, weak forces permit higher prices and above-average industry profitability. Firms can influence the five forces through the strategies they pursue. But some innovations can lead to a short-term advantage which, when every player in the industry is forced to follow suit, can result in the whole industry being worse off. For example, the first firm to advertise on television may gain an increase in market share; then everyone else follows resulting in a stalemate with the only winners being the advertising agencies and the television companies.

The crucial question, then, in determining profitability is whether firms in the industry can capture and retain the value they create for buyers, or whether this value is lost to others in fending off competition. Industry structure determines who captures the value as explained in the list below (which also summarizes this section):

1. New entrants compete away value, passing it on to buyers through lower prices, or they dissipate the value created by raising the costs of competing.

2. Buyers who are powerful are able to retain most of the value created for themselves.

3. Substitutes place a ceiling on prices (because buyers will switch if prices become high enough).

4. Suppliers that are powerful can appropriate the value created for buyers – it is passed from buyer to supplier with the firms in the middle taking only a small proportion.

5. Rivalry, like entry, results either in value being passed on to buyers (in the form of lower prices) or it raises the costs of competing (e.g. enhanced plant, new product development, advertising, larger salesforces).

When we look at successful firms we need to recognize that a large part of their success may stem directly from the attractiveness of their industry, rather than from the strategic brilliance of the management. Where demand is outstripping supply, and where entry is difficult, even the most mediocre management teams should be able to run profitable businesses. And if the business environment generally is favourable (leading to expanding demand) then there are likely to be many 'attractive' industries.

Looking into the future

The analysis we have undertaken provides useful insights into the structure of an industry, but it is more valuable to be able to look ahead, to predict how these forces might change in the future. What we have is a 'snapshot' of the industry's structure at one point in time; what we need to do is to inject a dynamic element into the model. Figure 2.2 tries to depict this dynamic approach.

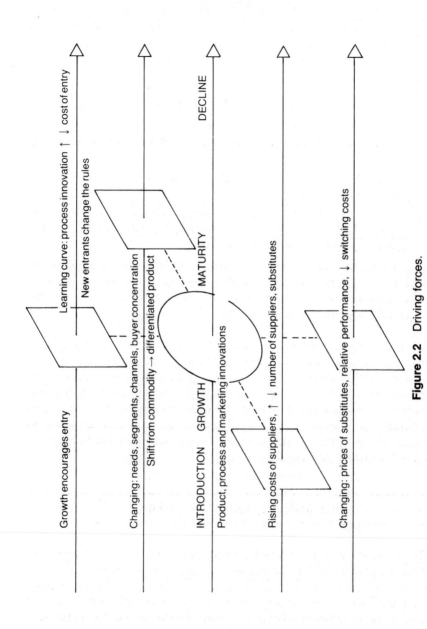

Figure 2.2 Driving forces.

33

Industry life cycle

The stage of an industry's development (its life cycle) can influence the nature of the competitive rivalry. For instance, in the early days of a new industry there are usually many new entrants. They are joining a growing industry where demand is outstripping supply, consequently the firms can meet their growth aspirations without poaching customers from rival firms. In this emergent phase there are no 'rules of the game', which means that a wide variety of products are on offer made by many different processes, some firms advertising heavily, others relying on their access to distribution channels to push the product into the marketplace. Often market share gained in the early stages of an industry's development can reap rich rewards later on, especially if there are advantages to be had from gaining experience faster than the competition. However, this assumes that the basis of competition remains the same; if it changes (e.g. from a strong emphasis on manufacturing experience to keep costs down, to a new emphasis on the importance of marketing sophistication) then these advantages are considerably reduced.

As the industry starts to mature, 'rules' are accepted and understood, consumer expectations about quality and performance are recognized and industry standards are established. Competition, in the transition to maturity, can become more intense as rapid growth can now only be achieved by capturing customers from rival firms. Cumulative experience no longer provides an important advantage to one firm because all firms have now gained the advantages of experience. A major feature of maturing industries is the tendency for competition to be based on price as firms' product offerings tend to become similar and attempts at innovation soon get copied.

In declining industries only the most efficient firms can earn reasonable profits; the marginal players are sifted out of the industry. Where there are high exit barriers rivalry can become intense as marginal firms hang on, leading to chronic over-capacity.

Interrelationships between the five forces

A change in one of the five forces can have an impact upon another. Imagine a situation where a technological breakthrough makes entry into the industry much easier. If the industry is earning above-average profits, new firms are likely to enter. This in turn could make rivalry more intense, and may well feed through to the buyers who are now better able to play one firm off against another. All these forces, then, are interconnected: changes in one are likely to affect the others.

There is another important point to note here. In any industry there are usually only one or two forces that are critical in determining industry profitability. For instance, in some industries the key issue is the power of the buyers (e.g. selling into supermarket chains or into the Ministry of Defence); in others it may well be powerful suppliers that extract most of the value from the industry. So in determining strategy firms need to take account of the critical force or forces and try to position themselves more favourably than their rivals.

Forecasting changes

Forecasting is notoriously difficult. One way of tackling the problem is to look at environmental *trends*. The wider environment in which the firm and its industry are located can be subdivided for forecasting purposes into four sectors:

- Political environment.
- Economic environment.
- Social environment.
- Technological environment.

Known as PEST or STEP analysis, this technique can be useful if it encourages us to think more broadly about environmental influences on the firm. Some examples of trends and changes in the four subenvironments are given in Figure 2.3.

However, even if we can forecast that a given trend will continue (e.g. increasing concern for the environment) it is often not at all clear how this affects our organization (see Figure 2.4). We can use the five forces model as an intermediate step between the wider macro-environment and the firm. What we can do is to speculate how trends might affect each of the five forces.

If we stick with our example of increasing concern for the environment, we could see how this may influence the five forces of the car-manufacturing industry:

1. *Rivalry*. Being 'green' and proving that you are so becomes a selling point in the first instance. Then the traditional rules of the

game change as other firms adopt green policies. Eventually, if you're *not* green you are at a *disadvantage*.

2. *Power of buyers*. Lobbies and pressure groups influence buyers.

3. *Entry*. Compliance with regulations sets up new entry barriers. But there are opportunities for new entrants to supply price-insensitive, ecologically concerned customers.

4. *Power of suppliers*. Some lose power over the industry some gain (e.g. the makers of catalytic converters).

5. *Substitutes*. There may be a backlash against the car as environmentally unfriendly; pedal power and public transport become more attractive.

Political trends?	Economic trends?
A Labour government	Monetary union
Tougher legislation to protect the environment	Exchange rates linked to Deutschmark
Resurgence of trade unions	Rising inflation
Break up of the USSR	Decline of the arms industry
Unified Germany	
End of the Cold War	Shift of financial power to Frankfurt
Social trends?	**Technological trends?**
Skill shortages: emergence of alternative labour markets	Increasing number of oil tanker disasters
Emergence of 'anti-growth' values	Massive development of public transport
Migration of skilled labour to southern France/Spain	Replacements for steel in cars, appliances
Increase in home working	Cure for common cold
Boom in leisure industries	

Figure 2.3 Some possible future trends in the wider environment.

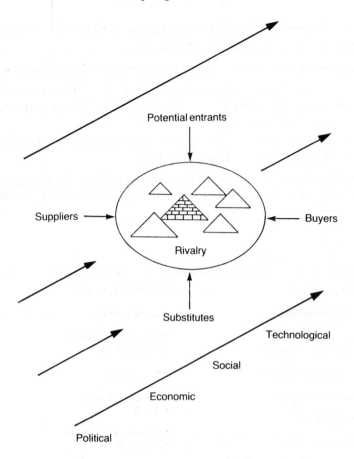

Figure 2.4 Environmental trends and industry structure.

Why do all this analysis and why bother to speculate about an uncertain future? If you understand the competitive dynamics of your industry you can then think about how to change things, or how best to manoeuvre the organization to deal with the threats and take up the opportunities that may be emerging. Either the firm can adapt to the changing conditions, or the firm can act to change the forces of competition. We see in the next chapter how this may be done.

'Forewarned is forearmed': if your firm is thinking about the future rather more than the competition you may be able to anticipate developments that may leave the competition reacting to rather than controlling events.

Buyer segments

Before we leave the Five Forces analysis, we might usefully expand the power-of-buyers part of the model. In its most straightforward version, the buyers in the model are all demanding the same basic product from the industry. However, most buyer groupings can be broken down into segments that require a particular set of product attributes. As industries develop, new segments of demand emerge, existing ones fragment into smaller subsegments, and some segments wither away. And, if we define our industry narrowly (to include just the domestic market), new opportunities may be developing in the form of foreign buyers for whom our industry's products are becoming increasingly attractive.

If we take the watch industry example again, we can disaggregate the buyers by the types of *need* that the watch is satisfying:

1. Functional need predominates (these buyers are interested simply in telling the time).
2. An item of jewellery (these buyers are particularly interested in the appearance of the watch).
3. An expression of status (here the important aspect is the manufacturer's label and the fact that those people whom the buyer thinks are important know what the label means).
4. A specific operating requirement (e.g. divers, pilots, nurses).

Segmentation can be done on the basis of demographic and sociological variables like age, class, income, sex, etc., but these are usually only proxy classifications of underlying needs.

It may well emerge in an initial analysis of an industry that there are advantages to be gained from segmenting the broad industry, and then conducting separate five forces analysis for each segment. Defining the boundaries of the industry is not an exact science. My preference would be to break down the industry into as many subindustries as is useful, bearing in mind that you sell not to a 'market' but to individual customers. So, the more you lump customers together (and make generalizations about what they want) the less likely you are to be able to target precisely on the needs of each distinct group of consumers. However, if keeping the industry definition broad helps you to understand the competitive structure and the

Illustration 2A

THE CAR AS FASHION STATEMENT

Millions of Japanese consumers now view cars more as fashion items or adult toys than as a means of getting around. The ultimate expression of that may be plans of Wacoal, a lingerie manufacturer, to sell its own sports car, the Jiotto Caspita, in 1991.

Many cars are only driven on the occasional weekend. The consumption tax introduced in April has removed the tax bias against models with engines over 2,000 cc. Japanese buyers now want bigger cars. They also want smarter cars, not just boxes on wheels. As a result the market has begun to segment, with the fastest growing bits being 'speciality cars' (i.e. sporty models) and 'RVs' (recreational vehicles such as four-wheel drives).

'The customer we had in mind', says the product manager of Silvia, a hot-selling sporty new Nissan model, 'is a 27-year-old who takes his girlfriend out to dinner. When he drives her home, her father, who meets them on the doorstep, is about to tell his daughter her new man is too young. Then he sees the car, and changes his mind.' This fantasy is a far cry from the traditional image of the workaholic salaryman with his regulation white Toyota.

The Economist (21 October 1989).

---

underlying trends more clearly, then keep the analysis broad. Remember, these are tools not rules. (See Illustration 2A 'The car as fashion statement'.)

There can be problems in defining the boundaries of an industry, especially if we take an overly product-orientated perspective. There is a view that only the consumer can judge which firms are in competition with each other. After all, firms can only be considered as being part of an industry if the consumers perceive them to be offering comparable ways of meeting their needs. This is not an academic point; you may gain some interesting insights into your 'industry' if you care to tap into consumers' perceptions of who, in their view, is competing with your offerings.

Competitor analysis

Most managers think they know who their competitors are, and they usually reckon to know quite a bit about them. However, only a few firms seem to devote the time and effort required to gain a deep understanding of their competitors. 'Knowing your enemy' can help especially if you are able to anticipate strategic moves that the competition might make. A systematic examination of your competitors and their strategies will increase your understanding of the nature of rivalry in the industry. Thus competitor analysis can help to enhance the Five Forces model.

In this section we present a series of checklist-type questions that could be asked of your main rivals.

1. Examine existing and potential competitors. This requires a close scrutiny of the needs your products and services are satisfying, otherwise you run the risk of defining your competition too narrowly.

2. Basic questions that need to be asked:
    (a) What is the competitor currently doing?
    (b) What is the competitor capable of doing?
    (c) What drives the competitor?
    (d) What moves might the competitor make?
    (e) Where is the competitor vulnerable?

3. Specifically, we need to concentrate on four main areas to establish a comprehensive profile of our competitors:

    Future goals

    Assumptions

    Current strategy

    Capabilities

Goals

Analyzing goals should give us an indication of how satisfied our competitors are, how likely they are to make a move, and how they might react to another's moves. Such insights need to be gained at the business unit level and at the corporate level.

Business unit goals

1. Profits: do competitors take a long- or short-term view? Does the stock market demand immediate profit performance or is the firm able to take a much longer-term view (if, for example, it was privately held, or if the financial community is more prepared to take the long-term view, like in Japan).

2. What is their attitude towards risk? Are they prepared to run the risk of being the first movers in the industry, or do they usually wait until others have broken new ground before following suit?

3. Are they aiming to be the market leader? The technological leader? What are their attitudes towards social responsibility?

4. The status of functions can act as a clue to the firm's priorities (e.g. who reports direct to the chief executive officer?).

5. Control and incentive systems can also act as indicators of priorities.

6. The background of the CEO can indicate likely preferences.

7. The extent of consensus at board level. Does the board share the same views about the firm's future strategy?

Corporate goals

1. What are the overall goals and the performance of the corporation as a whole?

2. What is the relative performance of the strategic business unit (SBU) that is in competition with our firm?

3. Is the SBU central or peripheral to the corporation?

4. Are there shared values or beliefs? Is there a common strategy across all SBUs?

5. What types of executive predominate at corporate level? What are the reward systems, control systems and organization structure?

6. What are the corporation's diversification plans? What is the role of the SBU in the corporation's portfolio of businesses?

These issues are explored further in Chapter 7.

Assumptions

Can we identify any blind spots where there is a lack of reality in thinking:

1. What do the firm's managers believe about its position, its strengths and weaknesses?
2. Is there any strong emotional identification with particular products or policies?
3. Are there any strong cultural or national biases?
4. What are the founders' beliefs and shared values?
5. What beliefs do they have about future demand and industry trends?
6. What are their beliefs about the goals and capabilities of competitors?
7. Do they believe in the conventional 'rules of the game'? ('We must have a full line', 'decentralization is essential', 'a large number of dealers is required', 'customers won't pay for quality'.)

Further clues can be gleaned from:

1. The functional background of the CEO.
2. The types of strategy that have worked well for them in the past.
3. The rules of the game in the CEO's previous industry.
4. The advisors/consultants they use.

Strategies pursued

Here we need to identify significant strengths and weaknesses that the competitor has by asking the following questions:

1. What is it best/worst at?
2. How consistent is its strategy?
3. Will its capabilities be affected by growth?
4. How quickly can it respond?
5. What is the relationship between fixed and variable costs? Do they have high exit barriers (which may include a strong emotional commitment to their existing industry)?

What are the likely responses of the competitor?

At the end of this analysis we should be in a position to assess the likely moves of the competitor. In particular, if we judge the competitor to be dissatisfied with its current position then we should be able to predict the moves it might make. We should also be in a position to assess how vulnerable the firm is to attack, and how the firm may retaliate.

So, a thorough competitor analysis should help us to anticipate at least some future moves and developments in the industry. However, bearing in mind the scarce resource of management time and talent, competitor analysis should play a supporting role rather than being the starting-point for strategic analysis. To quote Kenichi Ohmae, a leading Japanese strategy consultant: 'You create a value-adding strategy not by setting out to break the competition, but by setting out to understand how best to provide value for customers.'

Bringing it all together: integrating the environmental analysis

There is a danger when conducting a thorough environmental analysis of 'information overload' leading to confusion and incoherence. On the other hand, restricting the analysis may prevent you developing the fullest picture possible of the future business environment. What are required are ways of bringing together all the related strands of the environmental appraisal so that an understandable (and communicable) picture of the future environment can be formed.

We have already explained how the Five Forces model can be used to integrate:

1. The macro-environmental analysis (PEST/STEP).
2. The segmentation of buyers.
3. Competitor analysis.

However, by linking in these analyses to the industry analysis we have added to the complexity of the emerging picture. Here is a suggestion which may help you synthesize all this information in a way that avoids the pitfalls of over-simplification.

Constructing scenarios

Scenarios are realistic descriptions of possible future states of the industry environment. It is usual to draw up more than one scenario so that strategies can be tested against a range of possible futures. For example, you might derive the following three scenarios:

1. An optimistic scenario (where industry structure and industry trends, competitor moves, and buyer needs turn out favourably in the future).
2. A pessimistic scenario (which describes the 'worst case' situation for the firm).
3. A 'most likely' scenario (which is likely to be somewhere in between these two extremes).

These three pictures of the future facing the firm can help to draw out the major issues in the environment. These critical issues will need to be addressed when we move on to formulating viable strategies. Clearly, there will be some issues that the firm can act upon directly (either to reduce a threat or to exploit an emerging opportunity). But many of the critical issues will be outside the firm's control, so strategies will need to be developed that will help to position the firm either to gain a competitive advantage or to minimize the potential damage deriving from the environment. The issues facing the industry in the future may be determined by one or more of the following trends:

1. The current stage of the industry's life cycle (early, emergent, maturity or decline).
2. The growth rate of demand (stagnant or rapidly expanding).
3. Changing buyer needs.
4. Innovations in products or production processes.
5. The entry or exit of firms.
6. How easily innovations can be imitated.
7. Likely changes in the regulatory environment.

In the next chapter we introduce some ideas about competitive strategies that can help the firm position itself to advantage in its industry. These competitive strategies help to defend the firm against each of the five forces of competition. We also pick Ohmae's theme of understanding what your customers really want.

CASEWORK

Apply the Five Forces model to the Workgear case study in Chapter 1. You will have to use clues from Workgear's situation and experiences to deduce what the structure of the industry as a whole is like.

3

Competitive strategy

As explained in Chapter 1, this book concentrates mainly on business level, or 'strategic business unit' (SBU), strategy. This chapter is concerned with competitive strategy at the level of the individual business unit; Chapter 7 deals with strategy in multiple SBU organizations.

The debate about competitive strategy was considerably advanced with the publication in 1980 of Michael Porter's *Competitive Strategy*. This landmark contribution was followed up in 1985 with *Competitive Advantage* which developed the basic ideas introduced in the earlier book. Prior to these books it would be fair to say that strategic thinking had tended to focus on analysis of the external environment and of the strengths and weaknesses of the firm. SWOT (strengths, weaknesses, opportunities, threats) analysis, as it became known, formed the basis of strategic analysis. Only after completing a comprehensive appraisal of the internal and external situation of the firm could viable strategic options be considered. These options would emerge from the analysis. Options could only be broadly classified as, for instance, diversification, growth, harvest (to maximize the short-term cash flow from the business). The way that the business unit competed in the marketplace could not be generalized, it all depended on the prior analysis. Good strategies should build on strengths and exploit opportunities.

The logic of this approach indicates that, as each firm will be facing a different set of opportunities and threats (Os and Ts) and each will have differing strengths and weaknesses (Ss and Ws), the strategies that result will be unique to the firm. Unfortunately SWOT analysis in inexperienced hands tended to generate long lists of points, and the longer the lists the cloudier was the emerging strategic picture.

Porter's major contribution was to point out that there are only two routes to superior performance: you either become the lowest-cost producer in your industry, or you differentiate your product/service in ways that are valued by the buyer to the extent that he or she will pay a premium price to get these benefits. Firms can choose to apply either of these strategies to a broad market, or to a narrow, focused market. These options are summarized in Figure 3.1. Let us look at each of these 'generic strategies', as Porter called them, in some detail.

Overall cost leadership

If you offer a product or service that is of 'standard' quality, but your costs are significantly lower than the industry average you will earn superior profits (see Figure 3.2). This route to superior performance requires that your product is *not* considered cheap or low quality by the buyer, because if it were then you would have to cut your price to sell it, and as you slash prices your cost advantage ceases to deliver superior profits (see Figure 3.3).

There are many ways to drive costs down whilst maintaining average quality, but some routes to low cost involve either moving down the experience curve more quickly than the competition, or increasing the scale of the operation to gain the maximum possible economies that large scale might bring.

Figure 3.4 is an example of an experience curve. Note that lower unit

		Competitive advantage	
		Lower cost	Differentiation
Competitive scope	Broad target	Cost leadership	Differentiation
	Narrow target	Cost focus	Differentiation focus

Figure 3.1 Generic strategies. (From M. E. Porter, *Competitive Advantage: Creating and sustaining superior performance* (New York: Free Press, 1985). Used with permission of The Free Press, a division of Macmillan, Inc. Copyright 1985 Michael E. Porter.)

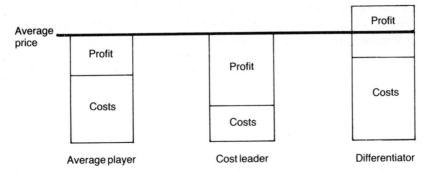

Figure 3.2 Generic strategies and profitability.

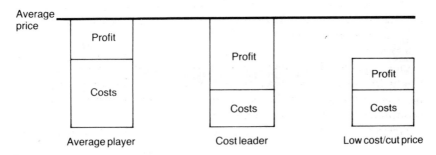

Figure 3.3 Low costs and cut prices.

costs are delivered through increasing the *cumulative volume* of production, i.e. doing the same things many times leads to finding more efficient methods of production. This is *not* the same as economies of scale. Figure 3.5 shows economies of scale in an industry. If you are producing at a small scale (point *x*) you are at a cost disadvantage with regard to the firm at point *y*.

The point about these two effects (experience curve and economies of scale) is that they imply that sales volume is an important prerequisite to the achievement of low costs. We can then infer that this route to superior performance involves grabbing and keeping a large market share. Therefore, if more than one firm is playing this game then competition for market share may well erode any cost advantages if prices are cut by firms scrambling for sales volume (Figure 3.3).

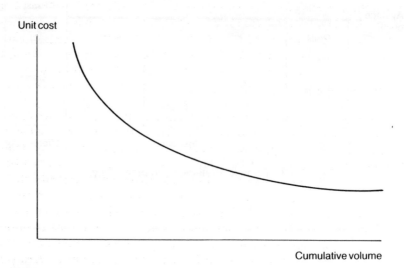

Figure 3.4   Experience curve.

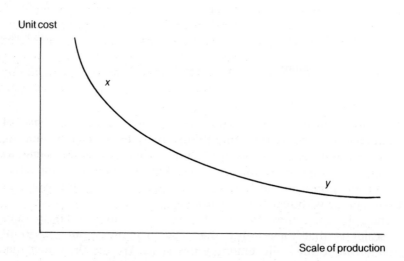

Figure 3.5   Economies of scale.

How does low cost give you a *competitive* advantage if your product is much the same as that of other suppliers in the industry? Low cost can enable the firm to compete on price if that was required. It can also generate profits that can be reinvested to improve the product quality whilst charging the same price as the average in the industry. So it is not low cost as such that confers competitive advantage, it is the consequences of low cost that improve competitiveness (see Illustration 3A 'Kwik Save').

Being a low cost producer should defend the firm against each of the five forces described in Chapter 2. Low cost producers are in a better position to survive a price war, and an awareness of this may deter higher cost competitors from competing on price. Pressures from buyers to lower price are likely to be weak as customers are unlikely to be able consistently to get a better deal from the cost leader's rivals.

If suppliers raise prices the low cost producer will not be squeezed as much as other, higher cost competitors. The firm's low cost position may well deter entry, particularly if the potential entrant hopes to compete on price. And price can be used as a weapon to ward off threats from substitute products.

There are some risks associated with the cost leadership strategy:

1. An over-emphasis on efficiency can lead to the firm losing touch with the changing requirements of the customer. In particular, in many industries the demands of the consumer have become more sophisticated and individual. The low cost producer who is dedicated to producing a standard, no-frills product may find his customer base is being whittled away by competitors who are adapting and developing their products.

2. If the industry truly is commodity based, then the risks of a low cost strategy are great. This is because there can only be one cost leader, and if firms compete solely on price, being the second or third lowest cost producer confers little advantage.

3. Many routes to a low cost position can be easily copied. Competitors can purchase the most efficient scale of plant, and, as industries mature, the experience curve effect confers fewer benefits: most firms have achieved all the learning advantages there are. But perhaps the greatest threat comes from competitors who are able to price at marginal cost in your industry because they have other, higher profit-earning product lines that more than cover the fixed costs of production.

Illustration 3A

KWIK SAVE

Supermarket success in the 1980s has been based on selling more products, more up-market, in bigger stores with more service. That message has been driven home as Tesco and the others have followed Sainsbury's formula and Marks & Spencer's products. Gone are the price wars of the 1970s. The piles of cheap baked beans and the plastic daffodil special offers. Instead we have fresh, chilled, chicken-in-polythene complete with listeria and high prices. Tesco takes credit cards and has won prizes for its wines. Asda boasts crèches.

The rules are clear. Make shopping exciting and you make money.

Kwik Save breaks those rules with the glee of a delinquent schoolboy. And makes plenty of money doing so.

Kwik Save sticks proudly to its highly unfashionable formula of selling limited ranges of branded groceries at lower prices than the rest, steering clear not just of fancy ideas such as delicatessens or in-store bakeries but also of any fresh produce. Cheap baked beans and breakfast cereals are its stock in trade – but only if they are Heinz, Kellogg's or the other market leaders. No own labels at Kwik Save. No nonsense about 'exclusive brands', as at Gateway.

Initially, this was because the range was constrained by the policy of not pricing products. Sticking labels on every tin and packet costs a fortune in store labour. So Kwik Save opted for a unique approach of checkout staff memorizing the price of every item in the store – just like real grocers used to do. But that required the range be limited to 1,000 items, which also helped to keep costs down.

Necessity was the mother of invention, then they made a virtue of necessity.

The policy is being watered down now, since the computers linked to electronic scanning can remember rather more than a thousand prices. But even so, the range will be limited to 2,500 items even in the largest stores, and those largest stores are still much smaller than the football pitches being opened by the major chains.

'No frills' is the promise. 'No nonsense' is the motto. So far it seems to be working, and as people feel poorer from higher inflation and higher mortgage rates it ought to work better still.

Because of its low overheads Kwik Save does not need the high sales and high margins achieved in the superstores. As chairman Ian Howe commented: 'We are happy for customers to come only three weeks out of four. They can buy their fancy food at fancy prices from the fancy stores of stars, so long as they shop at Kwik Save for the staples.'

The Guardian (1989)

Differentiation

Just being different is not a differentiation strategy. Offering the most unreliable and mechanically unsophisticated cars in the industry is not going to lead to superior performance. The key to a successful differentiation strategy is to be unique in ways that are valued by buyers. If buyers are willing to pay for these unique features, through higher prices, and if your costs are under control, then the price premium should lead to higher profitability (see Figure 3.2).

Central to this strategy is an understanding of buyer needs. You need to know what the buyer values, deliver that particular bundle of attributes and charge accordingly. If you are successful, then a subgroup of buyers in the marketplace (a segment) will not consider other firms' offerings as substitutes for your offering. You will have carved out a set of loyal customers, almost a mini-monopoly. This suggests that there may be several successful differentiators in a given industry. This is most likely where the buyers can be segmented into distinct subgroups who have particular, and different, requirements.

A successful differentiation strategy reduces the head-to-head rivalry found in commodity-type industries. If suppliers raise prices, loyal customers with low price sensitivity are more likely to accept the resulting price increases that the differentiator passes on. Furthermore, customer loyalty acts as a barrier to new entrants and as a hurdle that potential substitute products have to overcome.

However, the differentiation strategy is not without its risks:

1. If the basis upon which the firm seeks to be differentiated is easily imitated, then other firms will be perceived as offering the same product or service. Then rivalry within the industry is likely to switch to price-based competition.

2. Broad-based differentiators may be outmanoeuvred by specialist firms who target one particular segment.

3. If the strategy is based on continual product innovation (in order to stay one jump ahead of the competition) the firm runs the risk of breaking the expensive new ground merely for followers to exploit the benefits.

4. If the firm ignores the costs of differentiating then the premium prices charged may not lead to superior profits.

The term 'differentiation' is used widely in both the strategic management and marketing fields. It can, however, be used rather loosely to describe a firm's positioning in an industry. In most industries the firms do not offer precisely the same products or services as their competitors. For example, there may be differences in styling, in the distribution channels used, in the degree of after-sales support. If these differences lead to a firm being able to charge premium prices (i.e. above the industry average) then the firm is differentiating, in Porter's terms. However, in many cases these differences just give us an idea of the particular firm's positioning in the industry.

Because there are few pure 'commodity'-type industries, most firms in most industries inevitably have to offer something slightly different just to be in the game. These firms, then, would not be differentiators unless they could charge premium prices. This point is taken up again at the end of this chapter.

Focus

The focus strategy involves the selection of a segment or group of segments in the industry and meeting the needs of that segment better than the broader targeted competitors. Focus strategies can involve either being the lowest cost producer serving that segment, or differentiating to meet the particular requirements of the segment in a way that allows the firm to premium price. So firms can compete on a broad front (serving many segments) or on a narrow front (focusing). Both variants of the focus strategy rest on differences between the target segments and other segments in the industry. It is these differences that result in the segment being poorly served by the broad-scope competitor, who is not well equipped to tailor its offerings to the particular needs of the segment. The firm that focuses cost may be able to outperform the broad-based firm through its ability to strip out 'frills' not valued by the segment.

Broad scope differentiation and focus differentiation are often confused. The difference between them is that the overall, broad scope differentiator bases its strategy on *widely valued attributes* (e.g. IBM in computers), while the focus differentiator looks for *segments with special needs* and meets them better (see Illustration 3B 'Apollo Computers').

The obvious danger with the focus strategy is that your target segment may disappear for some reason. Either someone else comes in, 'outfocuses' you and steals your buyers, or for different reasons (e.g. changing tastes, demographic shifts) the target segment withers away. However, there is an attraction to the idea of targeting at a

Illustration 3B

APOLLO COMPUTERS

Companies like Apollo don't operate in markets defined by mass volume production, standardization of commodities and intense price competition.
   Apollo makes 80 systems daily, which are grouped in five families with 200 variables in each. They cost around £26,000. They field their highly specialized commodities in targeted, segmented markets, with sophisticated sales teams. And instead of heavy-duty layers of management and rigid enforcement of the separation of conception and execution, they cultivate their workers' commitment to their commodities.
   The company also unifies the workforce by designating everyone staff, sponsoring higher education, offering the same holidays (25 days) to everyone, providing free cancer screening, a smart gym on site and private health insurance. It has compressed the management structure, and assembly staff travel along the line with the computer they are making. A faulty product goes back to its producer. That generates its own discipline. 'We're all quality managers.'

The Guardian (16 August 1989).

---

narrow segment and tailoring your offering accordingly. If you get it right it makes for a good business. But, if you were once a broad scope player and you have decided to target solely at the higher value-added segments with a differentiation focus strategy there may be some nasty surprises lurking in the future.

If you have spotted the benefits of trading up and targeting you can be sure that others have seen the light too. Before you know it those price-insensitive, high-end customers will have plenty of firms to choose from, so putting an end to your price premium. As well as being attacked from the pricing side there may well be problems in store with cost levels. Shifting from broad to narrow targeting usually means a dramatic reduction in the volumes you produce. This can result in excessive unit costs if you have not trimmed your overheads to match the smaller outputs demanded by your narrower customer base. So you could end up being squeezed from both the price and cost directions.

Stuck in the middle

Porter suggests that the firm that has not made a choice about either being low cost or differentiated runs the risk of being 'stuck in the middle'. These firms try to achieve the advantages of low cost and differentiation but in fact achieve neither. Poor performance results because the cost leader, differentiators or focusers will be better positioned to compete in any segment. A firm that is stuck in the middle will earn attractive profits only if the structure of its industry is highly favourable or if the other firms in the industry are also stuck in the middle. Rapid growth in the early stages of the industry life cycle can allow these firms to earn good returns, but as maturity sets in and competition becomes more intense, those firms that have not made a choice between the generic strategy alternatives will be exposed.

Sustaining one or other of the generic strategies requires that the firm has some barriers that make imitation of the strategy difficult. Since barriers to imitation are never insurmountable, though, it is usually necessary for a firm to offer a moving target to its competitors by continually investing and innovating in order to improve its position (see Illustration 3C 'A New Year fire sale?' and 'Japan Inc.').

Assessing the generic strategy concept

Porter's contribution has been invaluable. He has raised substantially the level of debate about strategy. However, this concept of generic strategies is not without its problems.

We have already noted above that the cost leadership strategy

Illustration 3C

A NEW YEAR FIRE SALE?

Barkers plead with passers-by to enter Abraham & Strauss' new store in mid-town Manhattan, to apply for a charge card and spend, spend, spend. The desperation is understandable, and not just because A&S is the first big department store to open in New York for more than twenty years. Many of America's most famous stores – A&S, Bloomingdale's, Marshall Field and Sears, Roebuck among them – face the biggest upheaval in their history. The challenge for each is to find a retailing role

---

that it can perform better than anybody else. Those that lack a clear purpose and identity, as Gimbels did, will go out of business.

All of America's department stores are caught in a vice: on one side they are squeezed by speciality stores offering customers more choice and lower prices (such as Toys 'R' Us and Radio Shack, a chain specializing in electronics), and on the other by discount stores and European-style hypermarkets with scant service but unbeatable prices. The squeeze is tightened for some department stores by huge debts amassed in leveraged buy-outs.

Both Macy's and Marshall Field have deliberately moved out of the market for cheap merchandise, leaving it to the discount stores.

Sears, Roebuck's role as an updated version of the nineteenth-century general store – selling reliable but unstylish clothes and goods – looks increasingly antiquated. Speciality stores are luring away customers from even its renowned hardware departments. Sears' share of the paint market has declined from 42 to 18 per cent; of the appliance market from 46 to 32 per cent.

Several other stores have retreated from such unprofitable lines. A&S has only token furniture and electronics departments in its new flagship store in Manhattan; Macy's has all but conceded the camera market to specialist stores. Sears still tries to do everything and so does nothing very well. Its profits are stuck in a rut and it risks, like F.W. Woolworth, becoming yesterday's store.

J.C. Penney, once a near copy of Sears, has a much clearer direction in opting to become more like the American equivalent of Marks & Spencer. It is concentrating on fashionable, mid-market clothes, especially women's wear, and abandoning such relatively unprofitable lines as hardware and electronics.

The Economist (7 October 1989).

JAPAN INC. – STUCK IN THE MIDDLE?

'The strategic positioning that has served Japan so well in the past is no longer tenable. On the one side, there are German companies like Mercedes and BMW commanding such high prices that even elevated cost levels do not greatly hurt profitability. On the other are the low-price, high-volume producers like Korea's Hyundai, Samsung and Lucky Goldstar who can make products for less than half of what it cost the Japanese.

'The Japanese are being caught in the middle: they are able neither to command the immense margins of the Germans nor to undercut the rock-bottom wages of the Koreans. The result is a painful squeeze.'

Kenichi Ohmae, McKinsey Tokyo, 1987.

requires the firm to match the quality of the average for the industry. This is not a 'cheap and cheerful' option. If the product is seen to be substandard then low prices would be required to sell it, thus eroding the profit margin. Similarly, we noted that the successful differentiator needs to think about costs. In particular this firm must be ruthless about paring costs that do not feed through into something that is valued by the buyer.

So, whereas at first sight these two strategies might seem to be distinct and mutually exclusive, on closer inspection they appear to have strong common elements: both require a high concern for quality (especially as one route to low costs is to eliminate scrap and reworking), and they both require close attention to cost control. If this is the case it might be useful to consider these two not as exclusive alternatives but as *orientations* (see Figure 3.6).

A firm in position A in the figure would be pursuing an uncompromising differentiation strategy, serving a particular segment with a unique blend of product/service attributes, and earning a premium price. There is no great attention being paid to achieving efficiency: most of management time and effort is devoted to preserving and developing those strengths that have led to success, be it constant product innovation, unrivalled quality or rapid response to customer requirements.

The firm in position B is pursuing a 'pure' efficiency strategy. Efforts are channelled into driving costs down across the whole organization. There is little attention devoted to product/service development. Superior profits come from low costs matched with average prices.

The firm in position C is pursuing neither efficiency nor differentiation. It is Porter's 'stuck in the middle' firm. A lack of differentiation means no opportunity to raise prices above the industry average; and below average efficiency leads to above average costs. So, firms in position C are squeezed from both ends.

The firm in the enviable situation of position D has the advantages of both strategic orientations. The firm's ability to differentiate successfully leads to premium prices, whilst at the same time efficiency yields cost advantages. Firms in position D will therefore outperform others in the industry. Achieving both sources of advantage at the same time is difficult. Usually differentiation requires adding features which add to costs; and achieving the lowest cost position in the industry usually requires the firm to give up some differentiation by standardizing the product. But the greatest difficulties derive from the inconsistent and often conflicting demands on the organization that each strategy makes. We look into these differing requirements in the next chapter.

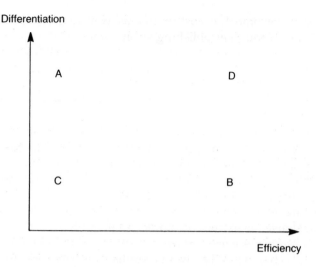

Figure 3.6 Differentiation and efficiency.

There are other problems with Porter's generic strategies:

(1) Why must you be the lowest cost producer in the industry? Surely, being second or third lowest would still yield above average profits? Porter's argument rests on the links between sales volume and the achievement of lowest costs. If there is a strong experience curve effect in the industry, or if economies of scale can be achieved only where one firm has a significant share of the market, then if two or more firms are seeking the low cost position a full-sclae price war is likely to result. The only winner would be the lowest cost producer. But, if these experience and scale effects do not operate to any significant degree, and/or if the firms in the industry compete on many non-price dimensions (like service, advertising, distribution channels) the disadvantages of being second or third lowest cost disappear. (We pick up this point again in the section headed 'Positioning the firm', p. 65.)

(2) There are other exceptions to the 'rule' that firms must choose either one or the other generic strategy. Innovation (especially innovation in production processes) can help a firm slash costs and differentiate at the same time. Also, if cost is closely linked to market share, then the low cost market leader may be in a position to enhance its ability to differentiate and still be the lowest cost producer. Alternatively, the successful differentiator may find itself with the sales volumes to enable it to become the cost leader as well (e.g. where the firm differentiates through establishing strong brands).

Buyer needs

What has been missing so far from this discussion of competitive strategy is the buyer, and in particular the buyer's needs. None of the strategies discussed above will succeed unless there is a group of buyers that wants the particular bundle of attributes offered by the firm. There is little point in pursing an extreme low cost position in the manufacture of mechanical calculators if no-one wants them any more. This is obviously an extreme example but it emphasizes the point that successful strategies *must* start from an understanding of buyer needs. Buyer needs change, as we saw in Chapter 2, so successful firms must continually keep in touch with their customers' needs, and anticipate how they may change in the future. Taking this line of argument a stage further, when we are trying to define the firms in our 'industry', the most reliable (and useful) starting-point is the customer's perspective. The customer's (or potential customer's) perceptions of alternative providers of products/ services that meet his or her needs might be rather different from the firm's perceptions of their competitors.

I'm totally convinced that the winners in financial services will be the ones that pay the closest attention to the customer. That means I have to say first, second and third, what does the customer want?
(Peter Ellwood, chief executive of TSB's retail banking)

Illustration 3D lists some ideas that can help in trying to get more information about buyers.

As industries evolve the nature of competition changes. 'First mover' advantages gained by early adopters of an innovation are rapidly reduced as other firms follow suit. For example, in chartered accountancy, firms started to explore how they might add value to the basic audit service they provide (e.g. by offering business advice to their clients). Soon after the leading firms began implementing this strategic move others jumped onto the bandwagon. The 'rules of the game' have changed; what was once a key feature of a successful differentiation strategy now becomes the *norm*.

As consumers become wealthier and more accustomed to quality, reliability and innovation, the standards in many industries are

UNDERSTANDING WHAT THE CUSTOMER REALLY WANTS

Do you know:

1. *Who ultimately makes the purchase decision?*
2. *Who influences the decision-maker?*
3. *What they are looking for?*

This information about buying influences must permeate every part of the business.

Some techniques

1. *Freephone numbers to encourage customer feedback.*
2. *Focus groups of customers tape recorded, and the cassettes widely distributed.*
3. *Good summaries of market research information widely circulated (see example below).*
4. *Managers from all functions to get out and meet the customer and report back.*
5. *Concentrate initially on the most important customers.*
6. *Cross-functional teams and meetings to air opinions and perceptions about customers, and improve co-ordination.*

Shops 'neglect service'

Mintel, commissioning researcher of the survey of 1,430 adults, suggests that the big chains have been so preoccupied with matching each other's prices and products that failings in staff training and after-sales service have gone unnoticed.

Only now, with customers complaining that there is too little to distinguish shops, are retailers likely to look for something else that can give a them competitive edge.

Given the investment by some big retailers in the campaign for Sunday opening, it was significant that the 18 per cent of customers who considered legislation crucial were outnumbered by those interested in children's play areas, baby changing rooms and toilets, and packers at checkouts. Faster supermarket checkouts were the main concern of 47 per cent of the sample. Fifty-nine per cent thought the introduction of knowledgeable staff offering 'real help' would be a key advance in shops selling electrical goods. This also came top of furniture store customers' improvement list and they also regarded speedy home deliveries at a time which suited them rather than the van driver as important.

Shoe-shoppers were particularly irritated at being pressed to match purchases with extras such as polish. One in four customers said rival shops sold the same style of shoes.

Caroline Dunn, senior analyst, says that the unique ingredient of shops ought to be the way they treat the consumer: 'All our research points towards a lack of awareness of the different stores, especially in the footwear, electrical and do-it-yourself sectors because they are so much the same. In our view, it is through levels of service that they can differentiate themselves.'

Sunday Correspondent (24 September 1989).

continually being raised. For example, in the early 1980s only one or two car manufacturers offered anti-corrosion warranties (e.g. Volkswagen/Audi). Now entering the 1990s the six-year warranty against body rust is a standard requirement. So constant attention to innovation and quality is a prerequisite just to stay in the game; it no longer distinguishes you from the competition.

This next section introduces Porter's value chain concept. This is a technique for analyzing the way the firm creates value for its buyers. There are mixed views about its usefulness: some managers have been able to apply the thinking to their own situations, where it has thrown up new and important insights into the business; others have even advocated restructuring the firm in line with the value chain categorization (e.g. for the purposes of management accounting). However, it is not an easy model to work with, and therefore this part of Porter's work has not so far penetrated managerial thinking to the same extent as his generic strategies.

Value chains

One way of gaining a deeper insight into buyer needs is through value chain analysis. The firm's value chain is shown in Figure 3.7. The value chain breaks down the firm into its strategically relevant activities in order to understand the behaviour of costs and the existing or potential sources of differentiation. A firm gains competitive advantage by performing these strategically important activities more cheaply or better than its rivals. It is worth, at this point, quoting Porter's definition of value:

> Value is the amount buyers are willing to pay for what a firm provides them. Value is measured by total revenue, a reflection of the price a firm's product commands and the units it can sell. A firm is profitable if the value it commands exceeds the costs involved in creating the product. Creating value for buyers that exceeds the cost of doing so is the goal of any generic strategy. Value, instead of cost, must be used in analyzing competitive position since firms often deliberately raise their cost in order to command a premium price via differentiation. (*Competitive Advantage*, p. 38)

The value chain displays total value, and consists of value activities and margin. Value activities are the physically and technologically

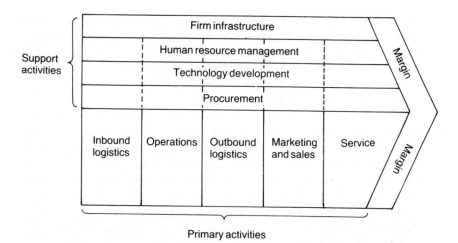

Figure 3.7 The value chain. (From M. E. Porter, *Competitive Advantage: Creating and sustaining superior performance* (New York: Free Press, 1985). Used with permission of The Free Press, a division of Macmillan, Inc. Copyright 1985 Michael E. Porter.)

distinct activities that a firm performs. Value activities can be divided into two broad types: primary activities and support activities. Primary activities are those that are involved in the physical creation of the product or service, its transfer to the buyer and any after-sales service. These primary activities can be divided into the following categories:

1. *Inbound logistics.* Activities associated with the receiving, storing and dissemination of inputs to the product (includes warehousing, inventory control, vehicle scheduling).

2. *Operations.* Activities associated with transforming inputs into the final product (machining, packing, assembly, testing, equipment maintenance).

3. *Outbound logistics.* Collecting, storing and distributing the product to buyers.

4. *Marketing and sales.* Activities associated with providing a means by which buyers can purchase the product, and inducing them to do so (advertising, selling, channel selection, pricing, promotion).

5. *Service.* Providing a service to maintain or enhance the value of the product (installation, training, parts supply, repair and maintenance).

Each of these may be a source of advantage, and, depending on the industry, different activities will be emphasized (e.g. in the photocopier industry service is critical).

Support activities can be divided into four categories:

1. *Procurement*. This is the function of purchasing inputs. It includes all the procedures for dealing with suppliers. Procurement activity goes on across the whole firm; it is not just limited to the purchasing department. Although the costs of procurement activity themselves form only a small proportion of overhead costs, the impact of poor procurement can be dramatic, leading to higher costs and/or poor quality.

2. *Technology development*. This embraces not just machines and processes, but 'know-how', procedures and systems. In some industries (like oil refining) process technology can be a key source of advantage.

3. *Human resource management*. This includes all the activities involved in the recruitment, training, development and remuneration of staff. Some firms recognize the potential advantage that can be gained through co-ordinating these activities across the firm, and through investing heavily in them (e.g. IBM, Unilever). The recruitment and retention of good staff has emerged as a major strategic issue for firms like chartered accountants and engineering contractors.

4. *Firm infrastructure*. This includes general management, finance and planning, estate management, quality assurance. The infrastructure supports the entire value chain (unlike the other three support activities, which can be particularly linked with one or two primary activities). The infrastructure can help or hinder the achievement of competitive advantage. An excellent management information system can help to control cost; a rigid departmental structure can hinder communication across the organization which may impede product innovation.

(Examples of value chains can be found in the Case Study appendix on pp. 144–5.)

Links between these value activities can be important sources of advantage. For example, good communication between sales, operations and procurement can help to cut inventory (of inputs and finished goods); the purchase of more expensive (but more reliable) equipment can lead to cost savings and quality improvements in manufacturing operations. Therefore, it is important that these activities are not dealt with in isolation; if each activity is assessed independently (e.g. on costs) important benefits like these may not be realized.

Links between the firm's and the buyer's value chains can be important sources of either cost reduction or differentiation. If the firm is supplying products or services to another firm (rather than the final customer) it is worthwhile trying to construct a value chain for the buyers' organization. The more we understand about our customers' business the better able we will be to demonstrate how we can help them to enhance *their* performance. By tuning into the buyer's business needs better than our competitors we can set up linkages with our buyers that make it costly for them to shift their business away from us. These switching costs can be real, tangible costs or they can be perceived inconvenience.

The value chain can also be useful in helping distinguish between the things we do that help to differentiate, and those features of our product/service that are merely different. For example, many computer manufacturers have invested heavily in speeding up their microcomputers so that processing speed has become a basis for competing in the industry. But is speed valued by all customers? It is, presumably, important for some buyers, but for others it may be irrelevant. The value chain can help us analyze the buyers' needs so we can make better judgements about what the buyer really values; and it can help us see where the costs of differentiation really are in our firm. This could help us decide where we might trim out costly features that are not highly valued by particular customer groups.

One important conclusion that emerges from using the value chain to analyze generic strategies is that different strategies (e.g. innovative differentiation, cost leadership) require different skills and resources. We explore the organizational implications of various strategies in the next chapter.

Positioning the firm

This section links together three themes that have been explored so far:

1. The firm's industry structure.
2. The needs of the customer.
3. Generic strategies.

The vertical axis of Figure 3.8 refers to the characteristics of a customer group or segment. Three broad segments are indicated in the diagram:

Segment 1   People in this segment demand a standard product, and they are very price sensitive.

Segment 2   These customers want something a little different from the basic 'commodity' demanded by segment 1. Customers in segment 2 are less price sensitive than those in segment 1 and are prepared to pay a little more to the firm that can tailor its products/services to meet their particular requirements.

Segment 3   This group is prepared to pay for uniqueness, innovation, exclusiveness. They are (almost) insensitive to price.

The horizontal axis in Figure 3.8 refers to the firm's position in its industry. This extends the ideas about analyzing industry attractiveness developed in Chapter 2 to the situation of an individual firm. Just

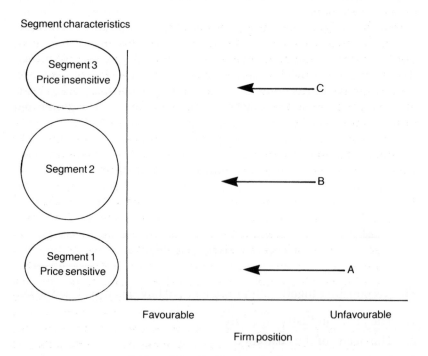

Figure 3.8   Positioning the firm.

as we can determine the relative attractiveness of a whole industry, we can use the same categories (the five forces) to assess the position of a firm within that industry.

A favourable position for a firm would be one where most of the following conditions obtained:

1. The firm has loyal customers.
2. Suppliers are not in a position to restrict supply nor bid up prices.
3. Other firms within the industry (or, indeed, from outside the industry) find it difficult to poach the firm's customers.
4. The firm has low costs relative to other firms in the industry.

Unfavourably positioned firms would not enjoy these conditions; they would be susceptible to threats from other firms, suppliers and customers.

A shorthand way of looking at industry position is to think of the firm as having its own 'barriers to entry'. These can be strengthened by improving the relative cost position of the firm and by carving out a set of loyal customers.

Firm A in Figure 3.8 has a poor industry position and is currently serving a price-sensitive segment. How can this firm improve its position? It may be that an analysis of the industry as a whole reveals that the prospects for this industry are most unattractive (due to, say, powerful buyers, declining demand, strong threat from substitutes, etc.). In which case there may be an argument for this firm getting out of this industry. (This begs the question of what industry could the firm profitably compete in. Answers may be thin on the ground.) Assuming that the underlying structure of the industry is sound, there would appear to be two basic options open to the firm:

1. Improve its position by ruthlessly cutting costs. This would then enable the firm to ride out pressures from suppliers' cost increases and buyers' demands for lower prices. If the firm were able to reach the position of cost leader then it might be able to compete on price, drive out some higher cost players and improve its position accordingly. One problem with this strategy is that the low cost position may be strongly linked to market share (due to scale or experience curve effects) but, when serving this segment, you need to cut price to get sales volume. If you lose this battle for market share you are likely to go out of business. So Porter's cost leadership strategy would appear to be relevant here.

2. Try to lock-in a subgroup of customers. This would be feasible if there was a group of customers wanting something a little different. These differences could be due to geographic location, access to distribution channels, or particular requirements like, for instance, needing delivery in bulk. Targeting this subgroup may not get you premium prices (so this is not a pure differentiation strategy in Porter's terms) but it may help you to set up real switching costs for your buyers. This would help to protect at least a part of the firm's customer base from attack. This is analogous to Porter's cost focuser.

Firm B in Figure 3.8 could try to differentiate by tailoring its products or services more closely to the requirements of a particular customer group. However, the price premiums available here are not likely to be great. Therefore, firms serving this middle ground of consumers need to pay a great deal of attention to efficiency. Large sales volumes may be needed in order to spread overheads. This may then mean that many subgroups need to be served, which, in turn, would restrict the firm's ability to focus exclusively on the needs of each subgroup.

Firms facing these broad segments need to offer something different to secure their position in the market, but this is not the same as Porter's differentiation strategy because only very modest price premiums can be charged. Are these firms able to pursue cost leadership? Maybe they can, but, by definition, as there can be only one cost leader this would seem to be a risky strategy.

So are these firms destined to be 'stuck in the middle'? Possibly not, because there are benefits to be had from improving efficiency even if the firm does not become the lowest cost producer in the industry. The risks of not being the lowest cost firm are much reduced here because the customers are not concerned only about price, and firms looking for efficiency would probably avoid getting into a price war. So these 'middle ground' firms would try to position themselves differently to secure or increase sales volumes rather than to seek premium prices.

Firms facing price-insensitive segments (firm C in Figure 3.8) need to emphasize strongly those features of the product/service that are most sought after by these buyers. Innovation or quality must come first; cost control and efficiency improvements take a lower priority. In this way firm C can strengthen its position by setting up high real or intangible switching costs for its customers. This can be done through branding, tailoring the product, establishing many links and dependencies between the firm and the customer.

In Figure 3.9 we have used the breakeven chart to simplify the strategies of firms facing these three types of customer segment. The low cost/low price firm serving segment 1 has low fixed and variable costs. This enables it to price competitively and still make profits at relatively low sales volumes. However, if the prevailing technology in this industry meant that there were significant scale economies to be had with large, automated production processes, then firms adopting this technology would have high fixed costs (but probably even lower variable costs). As a consequence they would need much greater sales volumes before they broke even.

Firms serving segment 2 need to invest more than segment 1 firms in trying to be different. This is likely to load up both fixed and variable costs. If they are not able to charge much of a premium price for these different offerings then they will need high sales volumes to spread these extra costs. The danger of carving out a niche too narrowly in this segment is clear.

Segment 3 customers are relatively price insensitive. They are prepared to pay for the added quality the successful differentiators are offering. Depending on the particular cost structure of the firm, and the extent to which customers will tolerate high prices, firms serving segment 3 can afford to carve out market niches. We could go further and suggest that without focusing a firm would not easily be able to sustain its position in this exclusive market.

If we take the airline industry over the North Atlantic as an example, our three segments might be:

Segment 1   These customers are looking for the cheapest way to cross the Atlantic. They are prepared to forgo flights at their convenience and in-flight comforts if the price is low. Students might fall into this segment.

Segment 2   These are the majority of business and leisure passengers who are looking for a little more comfort and convenience and are willing to pay above the basic price to get them.

Segment 3   These are VIPs who value flights at their convenience, speedy ground service, exclusivity and luxurious in-flight service.

Segment 1 would be well served by the 'pack 'em in' charter operator, operating out of marginal airports (to avoid costly landing and handling charges), and offering the minimum of in-flight service (bring your own lunch). All frills have been stripped out to achieve low costs and low prices.

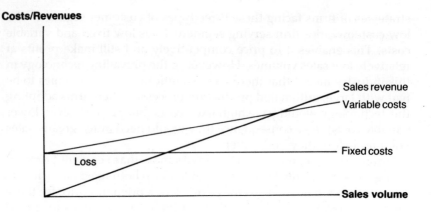

Segment 1 firm: low cost/low price

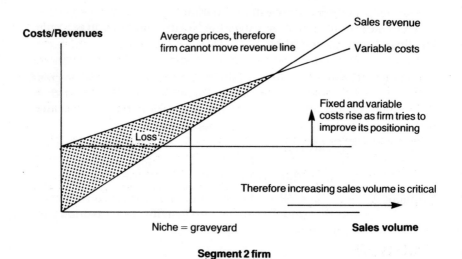

Segment 2 firm

Figure 3.9 Breakeven charts.

Competitive strategy

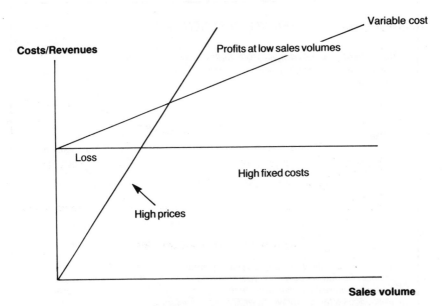

Segment 3 firm: successfully differentiating

Figure 3.9 – *Contd.*

Segment 2 is a large segment, and within this broad grouping there may be opportunities to identify subsegments with particular needs. However, we have said that these passengers are only prepared to pay a modest premium over the basic price. Airlines serving this segment need to ensure that they attract sufficient passenger volumes to cover their additional costs. These costs are added to by attempts at differentiation (see Illustration 3E 'Desperately seeking differentiation').

Segment 3 passengers could be served in a number of ways. They may be attracted to the first-class cabin of a regular scheduled flight (but they still have to mix with the tourist class so this would not suit all of them). Or they may prefer to charter their own executive jet. Better still, why not buy one?

CASEWORK

1. Clarify the needs of the two main buyer segments served by Workgear (the linen hire buyers, and the final user customers).

2. Which generic strategies are appropriate in each of these segments?

DESPERATELY SEEKING DIFFERENTIATION

The following are excerpts from airline advertisements.

On October 31st, Cathay Pacific launches the fastest Manchester–Hong Kong service. Just one stop in Frankfurt, then non-stop to Hong Kong. Join us in the fast lane and arrive in better shape.
Cathay Pacific

In days gone by, airline tickets were issued manually; a tedious, time-consuming affair. Today, we've revolutionized the process. Our computerized reservation and ticketing service is on a par with that of the world's leading airlines, allowing us to make your international reservations, confirmations and connections with just a keystroke. Hi-tech ticketing by gracious, attentive counter staff now ensures that all your travel arrangements are efficiently made in minimal time.
Kuwait Airlines

If, wherever you are in the world you want to feel in heaven from the moment you check-in to the moment you arrive. Fly the airline from the country that made travelling fashionable.
TAP Air Portugal

This year we shall once again be putting fifteen of the most modern aircraft into service. So that our collection will remain one of the most modern in the world. And we lavish all our care and attention upon it. With all that thoroughness and meticulous attention for which we Germans are famous.
Lufthansa

And Viasa brings it closer, on a flight that will be unforgettable from beginning to end, because everything is magical.
Viasa, the Airline of Venezuela

As an excellent gateway for international air traffic, Vienna's airport is becoming increasingly important. Its advantages: central location, short transit times, speedy check-in, close proximity to all departure gates and Austrian Airlines' convenient connecting services to Eastern Europe and the Middle East.
Austrian Airlines

We don't want you hanging onto the CALL button. We don't think it's necessary that you be kept waiting to have your wine replenished.
TWA

For the fastest route to free air travel, head northwest.
Northwest Airlines

Like JAL's new Executive Class with a wider seat which will have the world's first five inch personal video.
JAL Japan Airlines

When you fly First or Business Class on Delta Airlines, your flight attendant does a rather surprising thing. She calls you by your name.
Have you met her before? No.
She's simply doing what her Delta training has taught her.
Delta Airlines

Victor Amoussou, eye specialist, Dakar. He is known as one of his country's foremost ophthalmologists. A frequent traveller, he appreciates the fact that all of Swissair's aircraft are equipped with a special landing system for on-time arrival at the destination of his choice.
Swissair

4

The organizational implications of different strategies

Although there are some problems with the generic strategy concepts, there are, nevertheless, sound arguments to support the view that pursuing cost leadership and differentiation simultaneously is difficult. In this chapter we use the generic strategies to explore some of the organizational implications that may result from the pursuit of these different strategies. We begin by looking at the cost leadership strategy.

Achieving cost leadership

Assume that a firm is trying to implement a strategy of cost leadership. What type of organization would best deliver low cost products? In particular, what skills and resources are needed, what organization structure and systems are required, and what organization culture best suits this strategy? Most importantly, what should be the overriding values of the organization? Let us look in some detail at the requirements of a cost leadership strategy using the following organization categories:

1. Skills and resources.
2. Structure and systems.
3. Culture, style and values.

Figure 4.1 suggests that the strategy is *driving* the three categories so

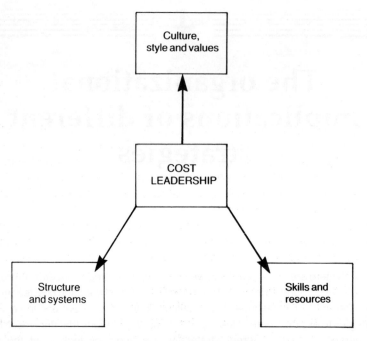

Figure 4.1   Cost leadership strategy.

that the organization matches (or fits) the strategy. (This diagram is based upon the McKinsey 7-S framework that you may have come across but groups some of their categories together, deletes others and adds 'resources').

We will assume, for the purposes of illustration, that our firm is manufacturing a product of some sort.

Skills and resources

Cost leadership requires skills in controlling the sources of costs: the cost drivers. Raw materials, power, components, labour, machinery or storage space could each be the single largest component of unit costs. These costs need to be identified and ruthlessly controlled. If the manufacturing process involves the use of expensive equipment it may well be that scheduling skills are required for maximum utilization of capacity. If labour forms a large component of costs (e.g. in a labour-intensive assembly process), then skills in method study, payment by results schemes, supervision, job design and manning are needed. Procurement expertise is vital to minimize the costs of bought-in material.

Critical resources might include capital (large-scale plant may be required to achieve scale economies), a cheap pool of labour, easy access to raw materials and an efficient distribution system. But above all, a cost leadership strategy requires skills at the top of the organization in managing costs across the whole of the organization, not just in obvious places like production. Moreover, if we analyze the firm using the value chain this may well suggest important linkages between value activities which if managed appropriately could be sources of cost reduction (e.g. investing in training could help reduce costs of scrap and reworking).

We need to bear in mind here, that although cost leadership requires extensive efforts to improve the efficiency of the firm, the quality of the products/services cannot be neglected. As was pointed out in Chapter 3, the cost leader has to offer *equivalent* quality to the industry average if its cost advantage is to lead to superior profitability. In a way, the cost leader has to be at least as 'differentiated' as the average players in the industry. In many industries the average level of quality is being continually levered upwards, largely through short-term competitive moves by individual firms that are soon imitated. So the cost leader has to keep up with these continually rising standards. The risk here is that the concentration on driving costs down leads the firm into neglecting quality and innovation.

Structure and systems

The nature of the production system influences to a large extent the organization structure required for low cost production. If the system is a mass-production process utilizing a large labour force then the organization structure might look like Figure 4.2. We shall use this example to introduce a useful way of categorizing the different parts of the organization (see Figure 4.3).

There are several layers of line management and supervision connecting the top of the organization (which we have called the strategic apex) to the bottom (the workers in the operating core). These layers of connecting management are referred to as the middle line in the diagram.

Because most of the work in the operating core is highly routine and procedural, first-line supervision can be responsible for groups of up to

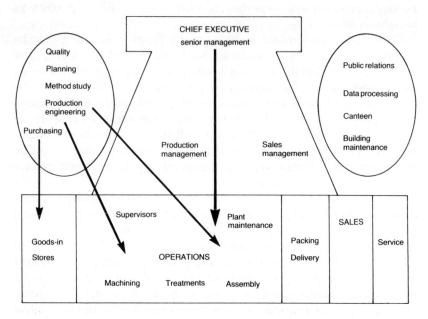

Figure 4.2 Organizing for efficiency.

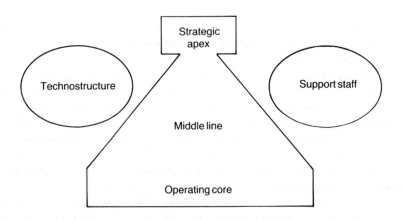

Figure 4.3 The five parts of the organization.

fifty operatives. This is because their work is controlled not personally by the supervisor but by a system developed by staff analysts (like work study engineers, rate fixers, trainers, production controllers, production planners or quality controllers). These staff analysts are not part of line management but they are highly influential and form a large and vital part of the mass-production organization (they are referred to as the technostructure).

Large-mass production organizations also tend to have another group of staff personnel, labelled support staff in the diagram. These include canteen staff, cleaners, building maintenance, security, public relations, legal, market research). Support staff differ from the analysts in the technostructure in one crucial respect: they are not closely tied to the main work of the organization, and because their work could be done by outsiders, they could be replaced by subcontracted staff. This makes the group rather vulnerable and relatively lacking in political clout within the organization.

So, the mass-production route to cost leadership leads to an elaborate and highly specialized organization structure. It is also a structure that abounds with systems: production planning, job descriptions, quality assurance procedures, job cards, budgetary control, standard costing, induction, appraisal, disciplinary procedures, etc.

As this type of organization has developed, more areas of decision making have been usurped by systems and procedures. In some firms the older line foremen, who can remember the days when they could hire and fire, discipline staff, recommend promotions and pay rises, determine the production schedule, make quality decisions, and generally *manage* the shopfloor, have gradually become disillusioned as more and more decision-making power has shifted away from them to staff personnel.

The five parts of the organization that we have introduced through this example (strategic apex, operating core, middle line, technostructure and support staff) can be used to describe any type of structure. However, different types of organization vary in the relative size and importance of these five groupings. We shall use the same categorization when we look at the structural implications of a firm pursuing a strategy of differentiation.

Culture, style and values

Unfortunately, too many mass-production firms have cultures that are more about conflict, deceit and fear than competition, caring and trust.

Size and specialization are partly to blame: the huge psychological distance between the top of an organization (the strategic apex) and the shopfloor causes misunderstandings and resentment. And the horizontal specialization into many departments and subunits, into line and staff tends to generate differing goals, outlooks, and subcultures leading to line-versus-staff antagonisms and mistrust.

Illustration 4A

TEAM SPIRIT

International Business Machines (now never known as anything but IBM) often seems to be more like a religious order than a business. Yet it is also a cut-throat competitor that dominates the world's computer industry. Employees enjoy lifetime jobs with in-built promotion and higher-than-average pay; in return they proudly – almost fanatically – do things the company's way. Tom Watson, who ran IBM at the turn of the century, sowed the seeds with his morning talks and his dreadful company songs ('Hail to IBM. . . To him [Watson] our voices loudly ring').

Oddly enough, however, the creation and development of IBM's personal computer took place outside the company culture. Previous attempts to produce a desk-top computer at IBM had failed, but competitors were becoming successful; so, exceptionally and with some uncertainty, IBM's management was persuaded to abandon the company's ritual of product development. In August 1980 it allowed an enthusiastic team in Florida to go off and build a personal computer. They did so in a year, and IBM immediately became a leader and standard-setter in a part of the computer business in which it had been nowhere.

James Chposky and Ted Leonis base their tale on interviews with members of the team, most of whom had left IBM disillusioned. The company had tried to 'fold them back' into the bureaucracy with only cursory recognition for what they had accomplished. IBM's views on the subject go largely unrecorded; the company did not allow its executives to be interviewed.

One can see why. The team's departures from the IBM tradition were dramatic. For the first time, the computer's operating system came from outside the company. Components were put out for competitive bids. The finished computer was sold not through IBM's own commission-driven sales staff but through Sears, Roebuck and Computerland. In the end, the company lost its loyal employees; but it gained huge rewards. Herein lies a tough, big lesson.

James Chposky and Ted Leonis, 'Review of blue magic', *The Economist* (22 July 1989).

Perhaps the most significant feature of this type of organization, though, is the abundance of routine, repetitive jobs found in the operating core. These jobs are rarely challenging and fulfilling to the average employee and, in order to achieve the efficiencies required in a cost leadership strategy, labour productivity must be continually increased. This is where many of the systems mentioned above come in; they are used to control the shopfloor workers and include machine paced work, job cards, PBR systems and the system of authority backed up by disciplinary procedures and punishments.

Management styles can tend towards the authoritarian, they are certainly autocratic. Values tend to emphasize controlling and checking, and efficiency. Secrecy, watching your back and covering your tracks can be widely shared behaviour norms.

This rather jaundiced account might seem exaggerated. To redress the balance we should acknowledge that some firms have managed to avoid the worst excesses of this response to mass-production organization. Enlightened management has been able to engender values that encourage commitment to efficiency and quality in a positive rather than a punitive manner.

So far we have assumed a mass-production operating core as the route to cost leadership. Some industries have automated their production processes to the extent that manual labour has been eliminated from the direct production process (e.g. oil refining). This in turn eliminates the need to control labour productivity as the main route to efficiency because with the automated operating core efficiency is designed into the plant. As a result many of the analysts concerned with standardizing and controlling work are no longer required, neither is a culture and style which emphasize control and authority. Thus automating the operating core enables the firm to move its structure, systems and culture towards a more relaxed, informal and meritocratic organization (see Illustration 4A 'Team spirit').

Cost leadership, stability and 'strategic fit'

There is little point in perfecting systems or automating production processes if the product being produced is being continually changed. So cost leadership strategies tend to be linked with *stable* environments. This also suggests that the products and services involved here would have stable characteristics: they are likely to be standardized rather than highly differentiated. So cost leadership strategies and the organizational structures that can best deliver them will tend to be stable, with many specialist staff and with quite complex systems.

The concept of strategic fit refers to the simultaneous matching of the organization and its environment. So our cost leader firm can achieve fit where its strategy of driving costs down through the introduction of systems, machinery and specialization matches a stable environment with price-sensitive buyers and predictable competitors. Moreover, there is internal fit as well, because the various dimensions of the organization described above are complementary (e.g. the drive for efficiency requires highly routine work, skills in production scheduling, effective control systems, autocratic management styles to help maintain discipline, clearly defined hierarchies and job descriptions, etc.).

Where the cost leader has automated the operating core entirely, internal fit is achieved around a different set of organizational dimensions. The highly skilled process engineers, control system specialists and industrial chemists work in stable group to run the plant, and group into teams to solve problems and introduce innovations. The structure permits communication across these departments (there are committees), the style is more open and the culture supports and values technical excellence.

Achieving differentiation

Let us turn our attention to a firm aiming to achieve superior profit performance through a strategy of differentiation. Taking the example of a management consultancy, we analyze the implications of a different strategy using the same organizational categories as when looking at a cost leadership strategy: skills and resources, structures and systems, and culture, style and values.

Skills and resources

Clearly our firm requires a high degree of competence in wide areas of management and organization. The firm may be offering a broad range of consulting skills and advice, or it might be concentrating on one or two specialisms (e.g. operations management or information systems). The breadth of services offered has implications for the types of skill required. A broad scope can be dealt with either by competent, adaptable individuals who can turn their hands to a variety of consultancy assignments (the 'craftsman' approach), or through the use of a number of specialists, brought together in project teams to tackle specific problems (the 'team' approach). The latter approach would require quite a large scale of business to justify the employment of many specialists (unless a more flexible option was feasible, e.g. subcontracting parts of the job to independent consultants).

Both the craftsman and the team approach require highly trained, experienced and thus expensive staff. People are the key resource in this organization. They need to be self-motivated and to be good team workers who are able to work independently on the clients' premises.

The firm needs to be able to convince clients that it can perform better than the competition not just to get business but to justify charging premium prices. So a deep understanding of the clients' business and its problems would seem essential, and the ability to communicate how the firm can solve problems (add value) is an important prerequisite to securing the premium-priced business.

Structures and systems

Flexibility seems to be vital if this organization is going to be able to respond to changing client needs. Decentralized decision making would seem to be an important feature, permitting the experts closest to the clients' problems the freedom to make decisions.

These two features will lead to a structure very different from the stable bureaucracy found in the production firm pursuing a cost leadership strategy. Opportunities for standardizing work are unlikely to present themselves as each client's problem will be in many respects unique. Clear reporting relationships (hierarchies) with well-defined job descriptions would also seem to be out of tune with the need for flexibility. And in an organization of highly skilled, independent-minded individuals often working autonomously we would not expect to find a strong management hierarchy with 'top-down' decision making. It would be quite difficult to draw up an organization chart for this type of firm because of overlapping project team membership, no clear line/staff distinctions and a limited management structure.

If team-working is necessary to carry out the clients' assignments, then this suggests a limit to the size of units. Project teams co-ordinate through face-to-face communication and this gets tricky when teams get to be large. So, even if the firm as a whole employs hundreds of staff, to deliver results they must be formed into many smaller units.

Figure 4.4 uses the five parts of the organization introduced earlier to depict this consultancy organization. Part (a) indicates the broad departmental divisions in the firm. Note that there is no technostructure, so there are no specialists engaged in standardizing the work, skills or outputs of the firm. There is quite a large support staff (e.g. secretaries, reprographics). There is a very short middle line, and the managers in the strategic apex become involved directly in consultancy assignments. Part (b) indicates the cross-departmental teams that are formed (and reformed) to deal with the changing assignments coming into the firm. The senior managers have specialized to a degree with some taking on the responsibility for marketing the firm, others looking after staffing.

Culture, style and values

How to describe this type of organizational culture? Rubber plants, first names, red braces and flexible working hours; meritocratic and participative; with expertise, problem-solving ability, selling skills, achievement and material rewards being highly valued. On the downside, these organizations can be highly political and can be quite ruthless in shedding below-par performers, where 'if you aren't moving up you're moved out'.

From differentiation to cost leadership

Perhaps it is unfair to use two such obviously different organizations to illustrate the organizational implications of the generic strategies (although the Workgear case study illustrates rather more subtle distinctions between these different strategic options). We would expect, in any event, a mass-production organization making components to look very different from a smaller service organization solving complex problems. But *could* a management consultancy pursue a cost leadership strategy?

Consider this plausible series of events. Our 'general practice' consultancy finds that it has been gaining a reputation for advising firms about installing quality circles (QCs). Over time successful implementations have led to new contacts through recommendations.

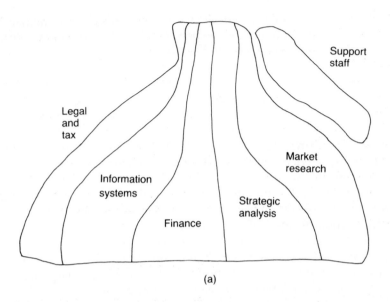

(a)

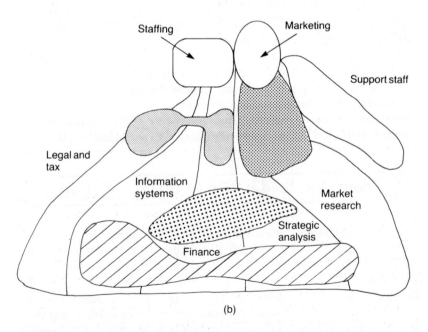

(b)

Figure 4.4 Innovative differentiation in the consultancy firm: (a) Broad departmental divisions. (b) Projects that cross departments.

More staff are recruited specifically to deal with this growing demand, and, at the same time, those experienced in the work have been refining their methods. Steadily, the firm finds that the majority of its business is stemming from QC and related work. They have now proceduralized much of the analysis and the training activities. They have materials, checklists, slide presentations, learning packs, documentation, staff to support the QC consultants and more administration.

Now, our firm is not alone in the QC consulting business, but through experience and sheer volume of work it has been able to standardize the service to the point where they can employ fairly inexperienced staff, train them in the methods they have devised, and send them, with confidence, into a new client's business.

This standardization of the service, coupled with their ability to employ less expensive staff, has enabled the firm to open up a significant cost advantage over their competitors. The service quality they provide is perceived to be the same, the prices they charge are also comparable, so the lower costs lead to bigger profits.

But there are other consequences of this developing strategy. The firm is now less flexible than it was; the newly hired staff are not capable of turning their hand to other, non-QC consulting work. The structure has changed from being one dominated by highly skilled professionals, to a mixture of general consultants, QC specialists, administration and many support staff (to maintain the systems, organize the training seminars, process the documentation, etc.). The organization has undergone a shift from a flexible 'adhocracy' to a more bureaucratic structure. This has been achieved due to the stability generated through the increasing QC workload.

From cost leadership to differentiation

What series of changes, then, might take place in a firm shifting from a cost leadership to a differentiation strategy? Consider the case of a commodity chemical manufacturer. Despite their best efforts to cut costs they are still unable to match the rock-bottom costs of the dominant player in the industry. They realize that, to match the cost levels of the cost leader would require a scale of operation that they would find impossible to finance because their relative cost disadvantage coupled with the low prices for commodity chemicals has not generated the margin that would attract the large amounts of capital required. So our firm is not the cost leader, but it has been playing out an efficiency-orientated strategy. All efforts have been on cost management rather than on differentiating the product/service to customers in an effort to justify raising prices. There appears to be a bleak future for the firm if it continues with this strategy.

A change in top management ushers in a new approach. What surpluses that have been generated are now used not to improve plant efficiency but to purchase small specialized chemical companies. Over time a portfolio of related speciality chemical companies is built up, and eventually the original commodity chemical plant is wound down and put in mothballs. Now the firm is in high value-added chemical products, and the organization has been gradually adapted to reflect this shift in strategy. Central office has been reduced to a small number of specialists more concerned with acquisition management than chemical manufacturing. Each acquired company is left pretty much to manage its own affairs in a decentralized manner. In fact, unless you enquired you would not know they were now part of another company. Funds generated by subsidiaries are ploughed into R&D (at the subsidiary level) and into future acquisitions.

The organization has been transformed from a large, centralized structure, into a decentralized, loosely coupled, almost holding company form.

Pursuing cost leadership and differentiation simultaneously

So far we have looked at firms pursuing *either* a cost leadership *or* a differentiation strategy, or firms adapting from one strategy to the other. Is it feasible to pursue both strategies simultaneously?

Take for example the case of a company like Toyota. For many years from the early 1960s they pursued a strategy that was essentially about driving costs down. Through this strategy they have been able to penetrate the world market to a remarkable extent. Note, though, that along the way they have had continually to improve the engineering and styling of their cars to match the increasingly sophisticated demands of the consumer. (If they had not kept pace they would have had to offer their cars at a discount.) Whereas in the past Toyota and other Japanese car manufacturers tended to follow the technological and styling innovations begun in Europe, now they are in many respects leading the way.

Our analysis, though, has indicated that the pursuit of efficiency requires a particular kind of organizational structure and culture very different from one that would be appropriate for innovation. Can these two contrasting organization forms co-exist? Some firms have tried to manage a production efficiency strategy with a differentiation strategy within the same organizational structure and on the same site. However, this can lead to problems, conflicts and compromises as the two strategies' requirements throw up contrasting imperatives: order versus flexibility, flair and creativity versus routine, autocratic management versus participative, control versus trust, etc. Compromising these two strategies as a way of dealing with these differing requirements can result in *neither* advantage (cost leadership or differentiation) being achieved. Porter's 'stuck in the middle' position.

Other firms manage these differing requirements by physically separating the parts of the organization responsible for delivering the differentiation component and the efficiency component of the dual strategy. For instance, a consumer products firm may locate its marketing and new product development departments away from the production facility. This, though, can lead to communication problems between, say, new product development and production engineering, but at least it enables the functions to be managed in the appropriate way (see Illustration 4B 'The BMW Z1').

Illustration 4B

THE BMW Z1

You'll see them on display at virtually every motor show.
All those gleaming glass fibre 'concept' vehicles built to show off the creative and the technical skills of a company's designers.
Yet destined never to reach the street.
Victims of the inescapable fact that it takes just as much imagination to get a vehicle off the drawing board as it does to get it on there in the first place.
BMW have put together a special unit to perform such tasks; the BMW Technik studio.
Here, a team of a hundred free-thinking engineers and designers function outside a conventional organizational structure.
A tight-knit group who took just three years to get the Z1 sports car out of the design studio and onto the roads.

BMW advertising copy

Two types of differentiation

Before we leave this exploration of the organizational implications of the generic strategies, it might be helpful to look at a development of the generic strategies concept introduced by Danny Miller. He suggests that the differentiation strategy be divided into two types:

1. Innovative differentiation.
2. Marketing differentiation.

Our example of the management consultancy would fit the category of the innovative differentiator. In order to stay ahead of its rivals the firm has continually to develop new approaches, packages, systems, etc. As a consequence the organization must be flexible, and may need a healthy turnover of staff to ensure the latest ideas are being brought into the firm.

By contrast, the marketing differentiator achieves higher prices largely through marketing efforts such as heavy advertising, promotion, a large and vigorous salesforce. There is no great requirement for product innovation: all the creativity goes into the marketing of the product. Many successful producers of branded consumer products would fall into this category (e.g. Unilever, Reckitt and Colman, Nestlé). There are interesting organizational implications associated with this strategy. The firm can adopt the dual structure mentioned above: the product (which is essentially standardized) can be produced in the most cost-efficient way, because this differentiator may well have the large market share that will enable it to exploit all the available economies of scale and experience. This part of the organization would resemble the successful cost leader.

On the other hand, the marketing part of the structure needs to be creative and innovative, encouraging, rewarding and retaining people with flair and imagination. It might make sense, therefore, to locate these characters somewhere else. The culture of the efficiency-orientated part may well spill over into this smaller, creative section with adverse consequences. Some marketing differentiators avoid these problems by subcontracting much of the creative marketing activity to agencies. We take up this idea of pervasive cultures in the next chapter.

CASEWORK

Given your analysis of the linen hire and final user buyers' needs, and your views about appropriate strategies to meet these needs, what, *ideally*, should the firm look like if it is successfully to compete in each of these industry segments?

Use the organizational categories introduced (skills and resources; structure and systems; culture, style and values), and pick out just the key features, not an exhaustive list, for each category. For the time being ignore the realities of Workgear: the firm is to be closely scrutinized in the next chapter.

5

Analyzing the organization

We have left the analysis of the organization's present situation until this point for a good reason. We mentioned SWOT analysis (the cataloguing technique of the firm's strengths, weaknesses, opportunities and threats) in Chapter 3 and that in many instances, the technique did not provide the strategic insights necessary to formulate good future strategy. The reason for this failure partly concerns the categorization of aspects of the firm as either strengths or weaknesses. Although often not asked explicitly, this technique begs the question: Strengths relative to what/weaknesses compared with what? In other words, on what basis are we judging that something is a strength? Are all the management team using the same yardsticks in their assessments? We have delayed the analysis of the firms' current situation until we have some fairly clear idea about what a successful performer in the industry should look like. Chapter 2 examined the industry environment and trends likely to affect the firm into the future. Chapter 3 considered strategies that can lead to superior performance, and Chapter 4 followed this up by analyzing what the organization would look like if it were to pursue a particular competitive strategy. So we have looked outside the firm, we have made some informed judgements about the future. We should now have some idea about what a 'successful' strategy looks like in the future, and how the successful firm needs to be organized to deliver that strategy.

Now we are in a position to answer the question posed above with regard to strengths and weaknesses, although we shall not use this terminology.

We can compare the requirements of future success with the reality of the firm as it stands today. This will give us a feel for the magnitude of change required if the firm is to move towards the successful positioning identified in the external analysis stage. We shall subsequently be in a better position to identify ways of closing the gaps between the required strategy and the present situation. And, then, we can prioritize these actions and allocate management actions to these priorities. We shall use the same organization categories introduced in Chapter 4 for this analysis: skills and resources, structure and systems, and culture, style and values.

Figure 5.1 suggests that the strategy of the firm is influenced and constrained by the existing structure, culture, values and resources. The reality of most organizations is that they fall somewhat short of the ideal or optimum set of skills, structure and values required to be a top performer in their industry. In this chapter we leave the ideal world behind and lift up a few organizational stones to see what crawls out. In some respects this chapter looks at the dark side of the organization, but it is essential that we develop a sophisticated insight into the reality of our organization. Armed with this awareness, and a vision of how we ought to look in the future, we can derive sensible and achievable strategies for change.

Structure and systems

Most organizations have structures that have emerged over time rather than resulting from deliberate attempts to design the ideal organization. However, these emerging structures should be reasonably efficient, otherwise the firm would have gone bust a long while ago. Because there is no ideal structure all firms suffer from weaknesses and problems that derive from the way people are organized. For example, as most firms grow they adopt a functional structure. This type of structure gives us the benefits of having specialists (in sales, production, engineering, personnel) but there are disadvantages that can stem from this form of specialization:

1. Different functions tend to have different ways of seeing the world. This can cause communication problems and can make it difficult to get all parts of the firm pulling in the same direction.

2. Each function has its own priorities, and these priorities can bring it into conflict with other functions (e.g. production prefers long runs of the same product, sales like to offer customers flexibility and variety).

3. Over time, these two combine to set up 'walls' between functions that make it difficult to achieve co-ordination and communication across the organization.

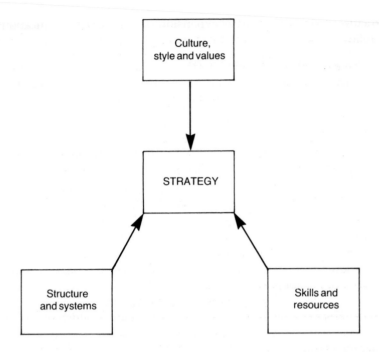

Figure 5.1   Structure, skills and culture restrain strategy.

Structure can influence the strategy of the firm particularly where one function tends to dominate the senior management positions. For example, a predominance of process engineers in the strategic apex could lead to an excessive concern with capacity expansion and process innovation which might be out of line with the needs of the buyers (e.g. for more specialities and tailored solutions rather than low cost 'commodities'). Structure can also reduce the firm's ability to adapt to external changes. Some organizations are excessively rigid, which hinders flexibility and can stifle creativity and initiative.

There is evidence to suggest that as firms adapt their strategies over time they tend not to readjust their structures to match the new strategy. Take, for instance, a firm that grows through the success of a single product. The firm then introduces new products into the same broad market to sustain the past growth rate, leading eventually to a greatly expanded multi-product firm. What tends to happen to the structure during this phase of expansion and product diversification is as follows:

1. The early phase of rapid growth is coped with through an informal structure, with little specialization (every one lends a hand to do whatever needs doing to meet customer orders).

2. This is followed by a professionalization of the firm as the need for systems and specialists becomes essential to cope with the expanding size of the business. Typically, functional specialisms emerge in finance and accounting, production, administration and sales.

3. The problems arise when firms stick with this functional structure as they become increasingly large and diverse. As more people join the number of management levels increases, resulting in communication problems up and down the hierarchy. Functional goals tend to leave no-one looking after the needs of a particular product or customer; people just do their bit and pass it on to the next department.

What tends to follow is a downturn in performance which seems to be the necessary catalyst that pushes the management into structural reorganization.

The key issue in organization is, having split up the task into specialist bits, to make sure it all comes together satisfactorily in the end. What is lacking in the over-large functional structure is co-ordination *across* the organization. There is a number of ways of tackling this problem:

1. Break the firm up into smaller business units that can focus on particular products, or markets.

2. Introduce staff who are responsible for co-ordinating activities across the functions (product managers, project leaders).

3. Formalize the role of the product/project managers in a matrix structure.

Generally, structural change is something that most managements avoid. It can create uncertainty, anxiety and resentment especially if it is badly managed. As a consequence reorganization is not only delayed but when it does occur managers tend to opt for structures that have already been tried (and succeeded) elsewhere. This idea is further explored in the following chapter.

Systems can help or hinder the implementation of strategy. In some bureaucracies staff at lower levels have to get approval from senior management for often quite trivial decisions or expenditures. If you grow up in this type of structure you are unlikely to feel comfortable about taking responsibility and exercising initiative. Job descriptions can be used defensively to avoid having to pick up new problems or responsibilities that have emerged due to changes in the environment. On the other hand, a lack of systems and documentation can lead to people reinventing the wheel, and to valuable information leaving the organization when individuals retire or move on.

Do the control systems measure what is important? Or do they measure only those things you can count? This is critical, because the control systems signal clearly to staff what the real priorities are. These things are measured, action is taken if you do not meet the required level of performance, therefore these things must be critical to the strategy of the organization.

Culture, style and values

A manager's perceptions of the world, like everyone else's, are coloured by his or her background and experience. So, when we try to inject some analysis and structure into the strategy-making process we need to be aware of the limitations of the individual manager and the management team.

Take, for example, the managers' views of the competition. These will be influenced by a whole host of factors, including comments made by customers, ex-employees, other managers, and by their advertisements, reported performance, as well as rumours that circulate in the industry. These snippets of information may well be 'interpreted' in the management team to fit a well-accepted, shared stereotype of a particular competitor. This could be based around some collective past experience where the firm either 'won' or 'lost' some battle with the competition. In some firms the competition are formally 'rubbished' by the senior management (although salespeople in the field might take a different view); in others there is a kind of collective inferiority complex, summed up in the saying 'the grass is always greener on the other side'. The point about this excursion into how people see the world is that perceptions critically affect the decision-making processes in the firm. 'Objective' information is ignored or downgraded if it does not fit the prevailing view of the world.

Strong shared values can be a tremendous driving force in the firm.

Peters and Waterman emphasize the central role values can play in their popular books (see, for example, *In Search of Excellence* and Tom Peters's *Thriving on Chaos*). However, values are deep-rooted phenomena; they cannot be changed at the drop of a hat, and we know very little about how they form, and how and why they change. Therefore, the values that pervade an organization would tend to be a stabilizing force, keeping the firm doing what it has done in the past, and is doing now. Problems arise if these values do not support the preferred strategy. For example, take the management consulting division of one of the major accounting firms. The dominant beliefs and values were:

1. 'There is safety and security in being big.'
2. 'We are professionals who are trained to avoid risk at all costs.'
3. 'Loyalty to the firm brings promotion.'
4. 'Partners know best, so make sure you check whatever you are doing with them.'

These beliefs and values are strongly reinforced by the training that staff receive, the role models around them in the firm, and the rituals and stories that form part of most organizations. But the preferred strategy requires risk taking, devolved responsibility and the exercise of initiative at all levels if it is to succeed. Interestingly, the person who acted as the driving force behind the new strategy joined the firm from outside.

Problems can arise where the management is determining strategy in a group or committee setting. There may be a set of unwritten 'rules' about how we conduct ourselves which could be harmful to good decision making. For example, it may be considered 'bad form' openly to criticize suggestions made by the managing director. It could be that the management team views itself as tightly knit and any doubters are clearly not 'team players'. Just plain fear or blind ambition can prevent people from speaking their minds.

In some organizations you find a predominant management style. This style gets reinforced where firms generally promote from within. Again, as with shared values, the style can fit the strategy very well, but in some firms the domination of one style can lead to problems. Consider the large mass-production firm which has an operating core comprising hundreds of staff doing routine, repetitive jobs. In many of these organizations you will find an autocratic style prevails. In some this takes the form of paternalism (or the 'benevolent autocrat'); in others it is expressed in the form of rather more unsavoury, authoritarian regimes.

The autocratic style in many respects fits the particular requirements of the mass-production firm. It centralizes decision making (which helps with co-ordination) and it helps to reinforce discipline on the shopfloor. You may not like this style, but there is no doubt that it can be effective. The problems arise when this style seeps into other parts of the organization where it is not appropriate, for example, the R&D department. Here it can be counterproductive if it creates conflict, resentment, stifles initiative and generally demotivates highly skilled staff who prefer to be managed in a less 'interfering' way.

How do you preserve islands of consultative management style in a sea of authoritarianism? Even if you believe participation is the correct style there are great pressures on you to manage otherwise. There will be pressures from colleagues (you would be considered as 'weak'), pressures from bosses ('you're not in control') and pressures from staff ('we don't know how to respond to this unfamiliar approach').

Lastly, cultures and values can become so entrenched in a firm that managers deny the realities of the marketplace and stick with the same strategy long after it was clear to those outside that the firm was backing a loser. Thus exit barriers are set up that prevent firms from leaving the industry (see Chapter 2).

Skills and resources

Most organizations would tend to approach an audit of skills and resources on a functional basis. In other words, the management would work through each function or department asking questions about what they were particularly good (and bad) at, and catalogue the various types of physical and other resources the function or department had at its disposal. This is all right as a starting-point, but it has considerable limitations as a way of assessing the organization's position *vis à vis* competitors and its ability to meet the present and future needs of customers.

Instead of this functional approach, we shall use a rather different set of categories to appraise the capabilities of the organization as a whole rather than as a set of distinct departments. We consider below various ways in which the organization can possess 'distinctive competence'. If the organization has no particular skills in an area, this may raise questions about whether or not this is critical to developing competitive advantage and meeting customer needs. If it is critical, then this must be a priority area for future development. However, if you feel that a more conventional audit would help your analysis, you may try approaching the audit using the value chain categories instead of the current functional or departmental structure you already have in place. This approach may throw up some interesting insights.

Economies of scale

Economies of scale can derive from many areas of the organization. Typically areas which tend to have a high fixed cost component (like advertising, management services, R&D) benefit most from larger-scale operations. Economies of scale can accrue in production, purchasing and distribution. In assessing the organization's position we need to identify areas where competitors are exploiting scale economies more effectively than we are, and areas that could yield useful economies that might give us an edge?

There are also diseconomies associated with large-scale production which may be important to the organization's ability to adapt, motivate its employees, serve particular segments, etc.

Learning and experience

Learning can reduce costs, and help the firm be unique. Questions need to be asked about whether or not the firm is exploiting the potential benefits of learning. Do we communicate ideas and suggestions effectively? Do we thoroughly document changes and improvements? Do we protect our ideas and expertise from exploitation by competitors?

Linkages

The cost and performance of one activity is often affected by how other activities are performed. For example, planned maintenance can cut machine downtime, higher-quality components can reduce production costs, co-ordinating procurement and assembly can help keep stock levels down (e.g. 'just-in-time'). One problem with functional organization structures is that these opportunities to reduce costs or improve performance are often missed because co-operation and communication across the organization are not encouraged. Links can be set up with suppliers and distributors to reduce handling and packaging costs and to eliminate goods-in inspection.

Response time

How rapidly can we respond to an order? How long does it take us to develop a new product? How fast can we customize a product or service to meet a customer's particular requirements? How soon can we deliver? How fast can we respond to customers' queries? Response time can be critical both to lowering costs and to developing a competitive advantage. For example, many Japanese firms have reputations for innovation which have been achieved not through original R&D efforts but through incorporating other people's innovations rapidly into their new products. Improving response time can reduce work in progress and inventory costs. There is evidence to show that the longer it takes to fill an order, the more expensive it is to produce. Lastly, how many orders have been lost due to a firm's inability to respond fast enough to the customer's requests?

Comparing the current position with the desired position

We should now be in a position to compare the actual situation of the firm with some idea about how the firm should look, if the firm is going to be a superior performer. In making this comparison I would recommend using some form of scoring system to judge the extent of the gap between where the firm is today and where it should be, using the categories of skills and resources, structure and systems, and culture, style and values. In carrying out this type of analysis it is important to focus on those areas that really make a difference to the success of the firm, rather than drawing up a long and unwieldy list.

Figure 5.2 shows a summary table which can be used to think through the issues involved in managing the strategic changes necessary. The scoring system that judges the extent of change can be quite broad, e.g. a score of 0 indicates that we already have this in place, a score of 5 indicates that a major change would be required to move from where we are now to where we need to be. The 'possible actions' column can be used to capture ideas that emerge during

	Ideal	Actual	Extent of change	Possible action
Skills and resources				
Structure and systems				
Culture, style and values				

Figure 5.2   Assessing the extent of change required.

discussion about how to make the required changes. They would need to be tested out and, most importantly, prioritized before any real action could be taken. We examine the processes of strategic change in more detail in the next chapter.

CASEWORK

1. Using the three organizational categories (skills and resources, structure and systems, and culture, style and values) assess the current state of Workgear. Concentrate initially on those key features of the organization that you identified in the previous chapter as being 'ideal' requirements.

2. There will be other aspects of the organization (good and bad) which are relevant to the firm's ability to achieve a shift towards the new strategy. Make a note of these: they will be taken up in the following chapter.

3. Try drawing up the summary table (Figure 5.2) for Workgear, indicating (using a simple scoring system) the extent of change required to move the firm from where it is now to where it needs to be.

6

Managing strategic change

Most firms do not require radical changes to their existing strategies, but they are probably not achieving all of their potential. The fact that any firm exists at all suggests that it must be doing many things right. But there is a big difference between mere existence and superior performance; and, just because the firm is here today, it does not mean it will still be around in five years' time.

We must also be wary of radical suggestions emerging from the strategic analysis which require the firm to move away from its present product/market position. The strategic problems of diversification are considered in more depth in Chapter 7. At this stage we need merely to think twice about any analysis which leads to the conclusion that we should get out of our existing industry into someone else's. I would expect that few people would reckon an 'outsider' could enter their industry and outperform its incumbent firms. However, many people do not consider it odd that they could move their firms into an unfamiliar industry (or take over and manage a firm in another industry) and expect to perform better than in the industry in which they have gained a vast amount of experience.

Although radical change is questionable, muddling through with the existing strategy is not the answer either. What is required is an informed view about how the firm needs to be improved and adapted to meet the challenges of the future business environment, and then, informed by this 'vision', management can plan the incremental changes required to move the firm in the right direction.

We began our analysis with a structured look at the firm's industry environment. This led into a consideration of buyer needs and an exploration of competitive strategies. Therefore we need to think about:

1. How best to meet current and future buyer needs.
2. How to achieve a superior competitive position.
3. How to defend the firm against the five competitive forces in the industry.

The essence of strategic management

It was asserted in Chapter 1 that the most scarce resources in the firm were management time, talent and commitment to make changes to the status quo. If these are such scarce commodities then we need to deploy them to best advantage. Analysis of buyer needs, competitive strategy and future industry structure might throw up a variety of problems that need to be solved and opportunities that could be exploited. We cannot do everything, and if we spread management resources too thinly we will achieve nothing.

A key issue here, then is, priority. Where do we start? A good starting-point might be to view the three strategic issues listed above as a definite hierarchy with buyer needs at the top, competitive positioning next and threats from the five forces third. The reasoning behind this is as follows. If we can identify and meet present and future buyer needs better than anyone else, if we can charge premium prices, and if we can control costs, then our margins will be well above the industry average. So, if we get it right with respect to the customer, our competitive position will inevitably be strengthened.

In turn, if we have a strong competitive position, and we are meeting buyer needs, the surpluses generated will enable us to ride out any threats from the other four forces. Profits and high margins can help us in a price war, they will enable us to cope with powerful buyers and suppliers. Healthy margins will help deter entrants (who know we could cut prices if we had to) and help us position ourselves favourably against potential substitute products. Moreover, satisfied customers will need a lot of persuading to shift their business away from us. By concentrating on meeting the needs of the customers we will have set up the 'local' barriers to entry that we introduced in Chapter 3.

We should try first, then, to direct attention towards the identification and satisfaction of present and future customer needs, rather than analyzing what we think the competition is up to. So strategy can be developed in such a way that those changes that will bring maximum benefit will be addressed first. If the firm is already well in tune with buyer needs then attention can be shifted to competitive positioning. If this is already as good as it could be, we might address other strategic issues emanating from industry structure, e.g. minimizing dependence on a single supplier or looking to develop new markets for our products.

Of course, most of these strategic issues are interrelated, and maybe it is somewhat artificial to tease out buyer needs from competitive position, and competitive position from industry structure. But none the less, if these are not addressed explicitly and hierarchically, at least in the minds of strategic managers, we run the risk of implementing piecemeal, *ad hoc* and undirected strategic changes. Such changes could jeopardize the integrity of the strategy, they could severely compromise and undermine the fit between the firm and its environment.

Judging the extent of change required

It is possible that the extent of the changes required to move the firm from where it is to where it ideally should be is just too great. It could be that the firm's competitive position has been so eroded (due to mismanagement in the past) that there is little point in trying to stay in the industry in the firm's present state. There are ways out of this situation (sell up, close), but they may be unacceptable. The industry analysis and the investigation of buyer needs in different segments may throw up other, less drastic options, where, for example, the firm shrinks to focus on a narrower range of customers (and products) where the firm is more advantageously positioned with respect to the competition. It may be necessary therefore to revisit the industry and segment analysis several times until a viable strategic option emerges.

Visions and missions

The general manager earns his keep if he or she can boil down all the information generated through a strategic analysis into a unifying, understandable, communicable and viable strategic vision. This could take the form of a mission statement. As was mentioned briefly in Chapter 1, these have become popular in some organizations, although there seems to be a rather mixed view about their effectiveness. The purpose of a mission statement is to communicate to those involved in making strategic decisions the broad 'ground rules' that the organization has set for itself in conducting its business. The mission statement should be broadly framed and it should act as an enduring statement of intent; it is essentially an internal working document, and it needs to be both concise and unambiguous if it is to be effective. To recap, a good mission statement might include the following:

1. A statement of beliefs and values.

2. The products or services that the firm will sell (or, better still, the needs that the firm will satisfy).

3. The markets within which the firm will trade.

4. How those markets will be reached.

5. The technologies that the firm will use.

6. Attitudes to growth and financing.

Good mission statements or 'visions' are inspiring and exciting. They need to be specific enough to act as a 'tie-breaker' (e.g. when it comes to the crunch quality is more important than meeting delivery targets), whilst at the same time it should be general enough to leave room for people to exercise initiative.

Where mission statements have not been effective it is usually because either they do not inspire people (for example, they merely consist of a series of bland statements that apply everywhere and nowhere); or they are not evidenced in the actions of the management. For instance, the mission statement stresses the importance of customer service and caring for the environment, but the managers' behaviour reinforces a different set of priorities, like cost control and capacity utilization.

The reason that mission statements are being discussed at the end of the book rather than at the beginning is that it is my belief that value from the mission statement idea comes firstly from the processes management has to go through in drawing one up. To meet some of the criteria listed the management team needs to address all the fundamental issues in strategy that have been covered in this book. Otherwise the mission statement will just consist of a series of empty slogans. So even if the mission statement ends up in everyone's wastebasket, there will still be beneficial effects resulting from the thinking and analysis involved in drafting it.

The second major benefit is the part it can play in improving the

Illustration 6A

THE PROS AND CONS OF MISSION STATEMENTS

Three labourers were working on a building site. A passer-by asked what they were doing. 'Breaking stones', the first replied. 'Earning a living', the second answered. The third allowed a greater sense of purpose. 'Helping to build a cathedral', he said.

The story illustrates why every organization should motivate its employees through a mission statement, argues Fred R. David of Auburn University in the US state of Alabama.

Mr David has recently carried out a study of the mission statements of

seventy-five of America's largest companies – but without acknowledging the scepticism with which many companies have come to regard such documents, especially outside the US.

Mr David is in no doubt that mission statements help to raise employees' horizons and that they can 'ensure unanimity of purpose within the organization.'

Mr David analyses the very broad mission statements of such companies as Rockwell International, the industrial conglomerate, and F.W. Woolworth, the retailer. He also cites the seven-item statement of New Jersey's Public Service Electric and Gas Company, which includes the immortal phrase that one of its purposes is to provide service 'at just and reasonable rates'.

What Mr David's building-site story and his study as a whole show is why most mission statements – those of the rambling American 'motherhood' variety, at any rate – are a waste of effort.

The virtue of a mission like the labourer's 'building a cathedral' or such real-life ones as President Kennedy's famous 'put a man on the moon', is that they are brief and clear enough to be understood by everyone involved and active enough to set a strong communal sense of direction. The same goes for Japanese statements of 'strategic intent', such as Komatsu's call on its employees to 'encircle Caterpillar' and Cannon's to 'beat Xerox'.

Few of the mission statements cited in Mr David's article, with the notable exception of Rockwell's, meet either of these criteria. Some of them probably even foster confusion among hapless employees.

Some people would argue that this is merely a matter of semantics and that Mr David has himself confused matters by suggesting that the labourer's cathedral-building amounted to a mission rather than a mere objective. They would say the same about Kennedy's space target.

Mr David tries to deal with this question by citing the brief 'motherhood' mission statement of General Mills, the big US food group, which expresses a dedication to the serving of four major constituencies: consumers, employers, shareholders and society. The company's chairman admits that 'the words become meaningless unless the statement is backed-up with specific objectives and strategies'. But he believes that the latter 'are far more likely to be acted upon where there exists a prior statement of belief, from which specific plans and actions flow'.

The trouble remains, however, that most such mission statements tend to provoke cynicism and confusion rather than clarity and commitment. If a company feels it must have a formal statement of values, it is surely better for it to express this separately from any mission statement. The 'mission' can then become what it should be: a clear, succinct statement of direction which motivates employees.

Financial Times (3 April 1989).

whole strategic position of the organization. This is a bold claim for a single sheet of paper, but a well-crafted statement that is understood and believed in can be a powerful force for change. An exciting 'vision' can provide the overriding framework within which management can exercise initiative. It can influence attitudes from the top to the bottom of the organization, but for it to be effective it needs to be a part of a much broader approach to managing strategic change in the organization (see Illustration 6A 'The pros and cons of mission statements). We now turn our attention to achieving change over a broad front.

Force field analysis

Figure 6.1 summarized the issues in managing strategic change. The analysis of industry structure, competitive positioning, internal resources, organization and culture have led us to a vision or view about what the organization needs to look like if it is to be a superior performer. We have also undertaken a thorough examination of the reality of the organization as it exists today. The question now is how to move the organization from where it is now to where we want it to be in the future.

Figure 6.2 depicts an old but well-tried technique called 'force field analysis'. The present situation is described in the form of a line which is subject to pushing and resisting forces. The idea here is that there are things helping us to reach the vision (pushing forces) and ranged against them are forces preventing us moving in the right direction (resisting forces). Now, if the pushing forces are stronger than the resisting forces we are already moving in the right direction. If they are not, then this suggests the amount of change required to reach the vision is considerable. This might warrant a rethink of the vision (i.e. we cheat and move the vision line closer to the present situation!).

Assuming that the firm is not in need of drastic, revolutionary changes we would expect the firm to be already moving towards the vision. There are three ways in which this movement might be speeded up:

1. Strengthen existing pushing forces.
2. Weaken existing resisting forces.
3. Add new pushing forces.

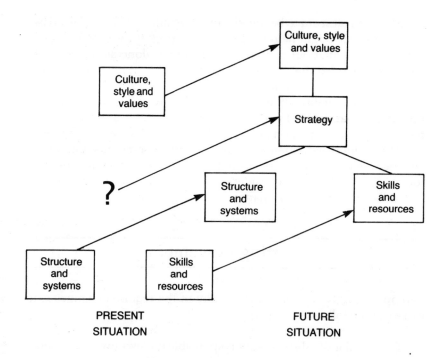

Figure 6.1 Managing strategic change.

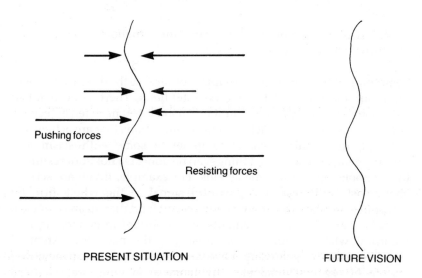

Figure 6.2 Force field analysis.

This might all seem to be merely an interesting intellectual exercise, but an example might help to illustrate the usefulness of the concept. Let us assume that our management team has done all the analysis, and has concluded that to strengthen its position in the industry, and thus to enhance the bottom line, the firm needs to improve considerably the quality of its products. Figure 6.3 summarizes the pushing and resisting forces. In order to improve the situation, to move the present situation more rapidly towards the desired organization, the team has decided to act to strengthen some pushing forces, add new ones and to work on reducing two of the major resisting forces. The next section considers how the team put these decisions into action to achieve real change in the organization.

Getting movement

Perhaps the only way of achieving any of the required changes is to carry out the following steps:

1. Clearly identify the manager responsible for 'owning' one or more of the actions that will push harder, or weaken resisting forces.
2. Give the manager the resources and support to carry out the action.
3. Set deadlines, monitor the developing situation and undertake corrective action where necessary.

Something of this nature has to happen otherwise the daily routine will drive out any poorly defined good intentions. There is no point in advancing on twenty fronts simultaneously: if you have ten objectives you have no objectives. Pick out important actions that are achievable and helpful as this is likely to generate some enthusiasm and commitment, and belief that things can be done. Do not underestimate the symbolic power of some actions. For example, if you are serious about cost cutting send a powerful signal to the whole firm by scrapping company cars for *all* management (and that means you too). Success and visible improvements are important in generating momentum, where, sometimes surprisingly, the pace and extent of change can then be geared up. Resistance to change is not an inevitable feature of organizational life. Involvement in decisions can be a powerful motivator, generating commitment to the agreed changes.

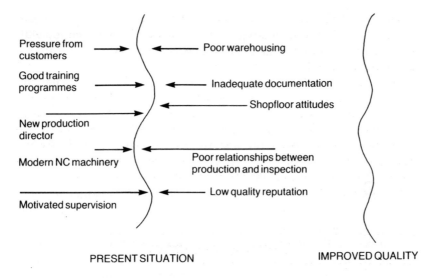

Poor warehousing

Inadequate documentation

Shopfloor attitudes

Poor relationships between
production and inspection

Low quality reputation

Pressure from
customers

Good training
programmes

New production
director

Modern NC machinery

Motivated supervision

PRESENT SITUATION   IMPROVED QUALITY

Figure 6.3   Force field analysis: improving quality.

To return to our quality improvement example, the management
team decided the following:

1. To attack their entire quality documentation system.
2. To take production and inspection staff away on weekend
    'workshops' to tackle quality-related problems.

Are merely two actions going to transform this organization? Probably
not, but at least it gets it moving in the right direction. The team
figured that the documentation system was a shambles, and until that
was sorted out they could not know from where the main quality
problems stemmed. Also, unlike 'changing attitudes on the shopfloor', they felt that it was at least something tangible that could be put
into operation.

The decision to take the production and inspection staff away to
work on quality problems should, they reasoned, not only improve
relationships between the two groups but also begin to throw up
suggestions and ideas to improve quality. Moreover, by having the
supervision and inspection staff come up with the ideas they would be
much more likely to be committed to implementing them. To move
things ahead the technical manager (who was in charge of the

107

inspection department) volunteered to get the workshops up and running, and the engineering manager set up a small group, with representatives from all the relevant departments, to tackle the quality documentation systems.

This example illustrates some important points about achieving change:

1. *Changes need to be underpinned by a clear vision* about where the organization is heading, otherwise you run the risk of introducing piecemeal, *ad hoc* and unconnected actions, and no-one really understands why things are being changed.

2. *You cannot advance on too many fronts*: this spreads management resources too thinly. The best thing is to 'bite off manageable chunks' of action that you know will get things moving in the right direction. Remember that even the longest journeys start with a single step.

3. *Responsibility for taking action must be clearly allocated* to an individual. The only things that come out of committees are people, so make sure that people know that they will be held accountable for achieving one specific part of the strategy.

4. *Intentions must be backed up by tangible, visible management actions.* Do not underestimate the power of symbolic events and changes.

5. *Involve people in working out how to make the change.* The more people that feel they have had a say in deciding how we are going to get to where we need to be, the greater will be the commitment to driving through the changes.

6. *Make sure that the measurement and control systems support the new strategy.* It is no good stressing that 'we're all about service to the customer', when you still measure and get worked up about budgets and excessive work in progress. If you are serious about customer service, you will need to work out not only what the customer truly values but also how you can measure (and reward) performance with respect to these requirements.

Dealing with momentum

Organizations have a strong tendency to continue doing what they have done in the past. This tendency is best described as momentum rather than inertia. Inertia certainly exists in some organizations, but momentum indicates a dynamic aspect to this idea. For instance, if a young entrepreneurial firm has a history of rapid growth and change, the people that have been there from the start may wish (or expect) this state of affairs to continue. So, momentum can exist in a very dynamic organization.

There are strong pressures on management to leave things as they are. If you change something and it goes wrong then, quite clearly, it was your fault. In some organizations it is not quite clear which aspects of their operations are responsible for the organization's success, therefore it is safest to leave well alone. Moreover, change is an admission that what we were doing before was wrong, and if change upsets status and power relationships there are likely to be as many losers as winners after the change.

Momentum leads to organizations delaying, until the last possible moment, organizational restructuring. And, when at last someone grasps the nettle, there is a strong tendency to move to a form of organization that is tried and trusted. There is a lot of sense in this. Organizations should try to achieve 'fit' with their environments. Moreover, looking inside the organization, there should be fit between the strategy, structure, systems, skills and culture of the organization. So these different aspects of the organization should match and support each other.

There is evidence to support the idea that, in practice, there is only a limited number of organizational types (or configurations) that are viable. Each configuration not only fits with its environment, it is also internally consistent: all the various components of the organization match one with the other. Figure 6.4 depicts the five most commonly occurring configurations. The ones on the left-hand side tend to be suited to simple tasks; those on the right are more suited to tackling complex tasks. Young organizations tend to start off either as *adhocracies* (if they are tackling complex tasks, like our example of the management consultancy), or as *simple structures* (if they are dealing with essentially simple tasks, like a driving school). The *professional bureaucracy* and the *machine bureaucracy* are particularly adapted to stable environments. As such they are not able to cope if the environment becomes increasingly dynamic. Our example of the efficiency-orientated cost leader introduced in Chapter 4 would be categorized here as a machine bureaucracy; a university or hospital are examples of a professional bureaucracy. The *divisionalized form* is appropriate where the corporation is dealing with environmental diversity (for example, in a diversified conglomerate like Trafalgar House).

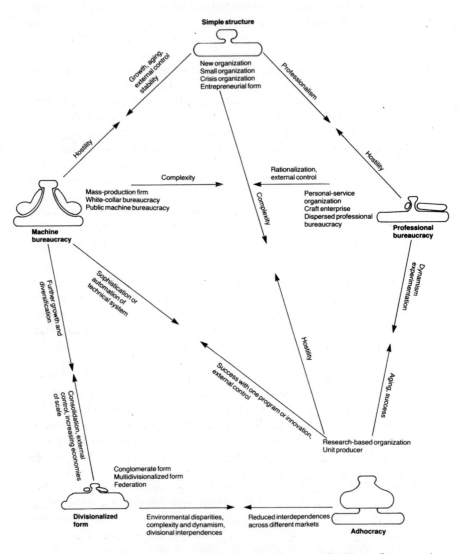

Figure 6.4 The five 'configurations'. (Adapted from H. Mintzberg, *Structure in Fives* (Englewood Cliffs, NJ: Prentice Hall, Inc., 1983).)

The momentum concept would suggest that organizations stick with their existing structure long after its fit with the task complexity and the environment has been eroded. Often it takes a serious downturn in performance before the organization restructures into the more suitable configuration. Some examples might help to make this point.

1. Let us take the example of the management consultancy introduced in Chapter 4. We can assume that the young firm began life as an adhocracy (very flexible, minimal hierarchy, few staff positions, informal). After a few years it finds it has settled on a limited range of services, for which it has developed a reputation. Many parts of these jobs have been routinized and are now carried out by semi-skilled staff. Report writing has been simplified to a standard format, there are more supervisors and managers around, people now have job descriptions, etc. This organization has, fairly painlessly, transformed itself into a machine bureaucracy. The tasks have been simplified (into, for example, a set of checklists) and the environment has become much more predictable.

2. A university is well established with a professional bureaucracy configuration (decentralized: much informal power resides with the professors and lecturers in the 'operating core', highly specialized, very stable). The winds of change blow away state funding. In order to survive the university needs to become far more responsive to the demands of industry, it must pursue all possible avenues for funding, more efficient ways must be found to conduct research and tutor students, aggressive marketing is required to attract foreign students. Environmental change has forced structural reorganizations: industry sponsors expect multi-disciplinary teams to be formed to work on their research projects; whilst, simultaneously, the demands of costs cutting have led to larger mass lectures, more use of distance learning material, the abandonment of tutorials. So the university is being pulled towards the adhocracy (to cope with the research needs) and the machine bureaucracy (to deliver lower costs per student). An awkward tension has been set up between these conflicting configurations.

3. One way out of the university's dilemma might be to adopt the multi-divisional form. Divide up the staff into teachers and researchers. Locate the researchers somewhere else. Design more efficient 'student processing' systems and procedures. Reward

staff differentially (researchers receive 10 per cent of every research contract they bring in; teachers get bonuses based on staff/student ratios). This splitting of the organization into divisions is one way of coping with the differing demands of tasks and environments. It has the merit of allowing each unit to adapt itself in all respects to its particular situation. As such, it avoids the compromises involved in trying to cope with conflicting 'pulls' on the organization.

Note that Figure 6.4 suggests that a hostile external environment (whether it be due to collapsing markets, strikes, withdrawal of funding, or a catastrophic accident) tends to force all structures to adopt temporarily the simple structure. This autocratic structure is essential to effect the urgent decisions and changes required to deal with the crisis.

The idea of having different parts of the organization serving different tasks is a theme that has cropped up in earlier chapters. Rosabeth Moss Kanter, a Harvard Professor, extends this notion in an interesting way. She talks about successful organizations that have managed continually to cope well with strategic change as having parallel organizations:

> An innovating organization needs at least two organizations, two ways of arraying and using its people. It needs a hierarchy with specified tasks and functional groupings for carrying out what it already knows how to do, that it can anticipate will be the same in the future. But it also needs a set of flexible vehicles for figuring out how to do what it does not yet know – for encouraging entrepreneurs and engaging the grass roots as well as the élite in the mastery of innovation and change. (*The Change Masters*, p. 205)

This rather intriguing idea of parallel organizations would seem to offer the benefits of specialization without the disadvantages that so often accompany it (e.g. inflexibility, lack of communication across the functions). The successful parallel organization looks just like a normal functional structure, but when a novel problem crops up, the additional interconnections between departments become clear:

1. Executive teams convene to consider decisions together.
2. 'Dotted line' reporting relationships come to the fore.
3. Multi-disciplinary project teams are set up.
4. Informal networks come into play.

The parallel organization, then, is able not only efficiently to deliver products or services on a routine basis but also to react effectively and constructively when new challenges and opportunities arise.

Research into strategic change

One strong theme that emerges from studies of strategic change is that organizations tend to go through long periods of stability interrupted by short periods of revolutionary change. These revolutionary periods are usually triggered by, for example, a serious drop in performance and/or the appointment of a new chief executive.

During the periods of relative stability the organization undertakes incremental change; gradual shifts in direction resulting from many small adjustments. Unfortunately, in some cases these incremental changes are not sufficient to keep the organization in touch with its changing environment. 'Strategic drift' occurs as the organization moves further away from the environment, until the point is reached where fundamental and revolutionary change is required to move the organization back in line with the environment.

Revolutionary change can be considerably assisted through the involvement of outsiders. These could be external consultants, new management appointed from other organizations, or management promoted from within the organization who are not strongly associated with the past strategy.

The leadership role of the chief executive officer is stressed in many studies. Successful leaders of strategic change create inspiring visions of the future; they live out their visions and support them with tangible and symbolic actions; they generate support and commitment at middle as well as senior management levels. As mentioned earlier, the vision needs to be at the same time broad enough to allow managers to exercise initiative and sufficiently detailed to convince managers that the leader knows what he or she is doing, that he or she understands this industry.

Not surprisingly, there is ample evidence to suggest that managing strategic change is a challenging and difficult task. Some strategic changes can be more easily implemented than others, especially if the change does not challenge the generally accepted views about how the firm competes. So, for instance, the dramatic turnaround in Chrysler under Lee Iaccoca's leadership did not involve a fundamental change in strategic direction. Iaccoca sacked large numbers of vice-presidents (and put his own people in their places), changed some systems, emphasized cost saving by paying himself $1 a year, and hired a new advertising agency. These changes reinforced or accelerated trends that were already around in the organization. It was Iaccoca's drive, energy and clearly articulated sense of mission that made the difference rather than the introduction of a new competitive strategy.

CASEWORK

1. Select the most attractive future strategy for Workgear based on your prior analysis.

2. Given this vision about how Workgear should look in the future, use force field analysis to identify the existing pushing and resisting forces.

3. Assess the strength of these forces. For instance, what are the two strongest resisting forces? What is the strongest pushing force?

4. How could the firm move more rapidly towards the vision? What pushing forces could be strengthened (and how)? What resisting forces could be weakened? And how might new pushing forces be added?

5. Given the scarcity of management resources, what should be the priorities for action? How can they ensure the changes happen?

7

Corporate strategy and global strategy

So far we have concentrated on strategy at the business unit level. In this chapter we move up a level to consider strategy making at the corporate level. Here the strategic issues shift to decisions about, for example, what businesses should we be in, and how should we allocate resources between them? These strategic questions become particularly important where a corporation has pursued a strategy of diversification.

The senior managers in diversified corporations face a new set of problems:

1. How do we manage a wide spread of businesses (especially as we probably know very little about how to compete in each individual business unit's industry)?

2. How do we allocate scarce capital between these diverse businesses?

3. How do we organize the corporation? How much decision making should we allow at the level of the individual business unit? What activities would benefit from being organized centrally?

4. How do we exploit the potential links between different, but related, business units?

5. How do we develop and reward business unit managers?

Perhaps the biggest strategic question facing the corporation is why is it there at all? What are the advantages to the shareholder of the diversified corporation? Does the value of the corporation exceed the sum of the parts? (See Illustration 7A 'Waiting for the barbarians'.)

We have seen over the past twenty-five years diversification as a strategy moving in, and then out of, favour. Many large diversified conglomerates were

WAITING FOR THE BARBARIANS

Sir James Goldsmith and two rich henchmen, the elegant Mr Jacob Rothschild and the Australian Mr Kerry Packer, believe good companies concentrate on what they do best. By this reasoning conglomerates are self-evidently bad companies, created by managements more interested in size and deep-pile carpets than value. Conglomerates pay a premium to shareholders in companies they acquire rather than hand it over to their own shareholders. Their biggest gains from acquisitions are the one-off kind that flow from kicking out an acquired firm's managers and eliminating waste.

Once such profit has been made, it soon becomes painfully clear that the parts of a conglomerate are worth more separately than together. Consider SCM, a conglomerate that Hanson, a recognized master of company break-ups, bought in January 1986 for $930m, then thought to be more than fair price for a troubled company. By the end of 1988 Hanson had raised $1.3 billion by selling all SCM's businesses except its core one of making typewriters. That is thought to be worth around $5 billion now.

It is in this spirit that the trio led by Sir James has launched an attack as much on the idea of the conglomerate as on BAT. 'This exercise is all about the defective architecture of very large companies', says Mr Rothschild. He should know. He built a financial-services conglomerate in the mid-1980s and then dismantled it. That begs the question: in what ways is BAT defective?

The burly Mr Patrick Sheehy, a tobacco man who has worked for BAT for thirty-nine years, has guided the company's strategy since 1982, when he was made chairman. His brief was straightforward: the tobacco business is stagnant but provides stable and strong cashflow. BAT, the world's largest tobacco company (Benson & Hedges and Kool are two of its better known cigarettes), was well positioned in the market. It has a near-monopoly in several fast-growing markets for cigarettes in poor countries. Mr Sheehy had to work out to invest Third World profits in safe First World economies. Like his peers at Philip Morris and R.J. Reynolds, he chose diversification.

With the benefits of that infallible strategist, hindsight, it is easy to say that shareholders would have been better off if the tobacco companies had just handed back their excess cash in dividends. But no management likes doing that: it is hard to keep staff motivated when they are just managing a declining asset.

Nor did Mr Sheehy fall for the honey-trap of synergy, unlike R.J. Reynolds, which bought Nabisco saying it could use its brand marketing

116

skills on food just as well as on cigarettes. Now Kohlberg, Kravis, Roberts, the leveraged buy-out kings, are busily unbundling the empire.

Instead Mr Sheehy bought into three unrelated areas – paper (Wiggins Teape), retailing (Argos-to-Saks Fifth Avenue) and insurance (Eagle Star-to-Farmers Group). Mistakes were made in the last two fields, and the whole thing lacked a little lustre. But it was an honest and thoughtful attempt to build businesses, and despite some past blunders BAT's return on equity is well above the average for British companies. The company's earning per share started to recover from stagnation between 1984 and 1987.

Then along comes Sir James with one fact that wreaks havoc with the logic of diversification strategy. Over the past ten years BAT has spent £7 billion on acquisitions. At the end of last year before bid speculation boosted the value of its shares, its market capitalization was roughly the same amount. The break-up value of BAT is at least £16 billion, probably closer to £20 billion. This steep discount reflects what the bidders see as BAT's basic flaw: 'The conglomerate that has been created makes no managerial sense', says their offer document. The way the market puts it is that Mr Sheehy and his colleagues are worth less than nothing to their company.

The Economist (15 July 1989).

formed in the 1960s and early 1970s, and the strategic logic underpinning them centred either on the concept of managing a portfolio of different businesses, or on the benefits of synergy. Synergy is often summarized in the textbooks as 2+2=5 (in other words, the whole is greater than the sum of the parts). Fortunately, for many advocates of the benefits of synergy, it is almost impossible to measure its effects (there is no way of determining how the individual businesses would have fared outside of the corporation). In retrospect, one cannot help but conclude that the drive to form some large conglomerates owed more to management egos than any strategic logic.

Some past errors in acquisition strategies include the following:

1. *Restructuring as strategy.* This type of acquisitive growth has been a particular feature of the 1980s. It typically proceeds as follows. An outsider buys up a sleepy corporation, fires the management, closes inefficient factories, screws down tight on overheads and suppliers, and thereby improves the profitability of the business. The problem here is what do you do next? You have sorted out the inefficiencies that resulted from the previous management's incompetence; but this has yielded a one-off, short-term gain. Where will the corporation gain superior performance in the future?

2. *Buying competitors*. This is another route to short-term success. This strategy can help you reduce costs (by spreading overheads), and it can improve the industry structure (by buying competitors you reduce competition, which may work through to improved prices and margins). But, as with the restructuring strategy, what do you do next?

However, we cannot afford to be too cynical. As any Hanson shareholder who got in on the ground floor would tell you, conglomerate diversification is a great idea if the corporate managers know their business. But the key issue is whether the corporation can enhance the competitive advantage of the individual business unit. If it cannot, the shareholders would be better off if the diversified corporation was broken up and the parts sold off. So the trend to large conglomerates has recently been superseded by the reverse trend: 'unbundling', 'demerger' and management buy-outs (and leveraged buy-outs) are now fashionable. We now have the concept of 'negative synergy', where a corporation's stock market valuation is well below what the individual businesses would yield if it were 'unbundled'.

Managing diverse corporations

The Boston Consulting Group's (BCG's) portfolio matrix is particularly relevant to diversified businesses. The Boston Box (as it is often affectionately called) was the first, and the most enduring, of the portfolio planning techniques (see Figure 7.1). Like SWOT analysis, it has had the misfortune of being easily recalled and improperly applied. The basic logic of the device is that relative market share is linked directly to cash generation and profitability. The firm with the largest cumulative volume gains the benefits of the experience curve first, so market share is critical. The vertical axis refers to the growth rate of the market at which each business (or product) is targeted.

Businesses with high relative market share and low growth require little investment and generate lots of cash (hence the cash cow in the bottom left-hand corner of Figure 7.1. Dogs have low relative shares in low growth markets: so there is little future in keeping them. Question marks indicate a follower positioning in a growth market. These businesses require large amounts of cash to turn them into stars. Stars are able to fund their own development because they have a leading share position in their markets.

The problem with all this is that it hinges on a rather crude view of the competitive positioning of individual businesses. Relative market

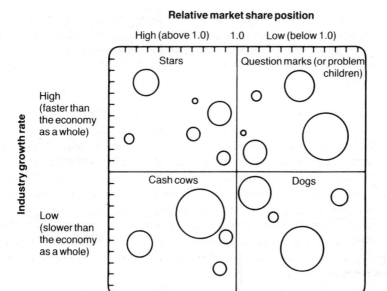

Figure 7.1   The BCG growth/share business portfolio matrix.

share is indeed important, and so is industry growth rate, but as we have seen in the earlier chapters, there is a wide range of other variables in the industry environment and in the way the firm is managed that have a bearing on profitability. This matrix takes no account of differentation or focus strategies; it seems to relate best to cost-based strategies where price competition prevails and experience curve effects are significant.

The basic BCG matrix has been extended and developed to incorporate more sophistication. But as the axes in these new matrices became more complex and multi-dimensional, and as the number of boxes extended (to, for instance, nine cells) the advantages of clarity were lost (see Figure 7.2 for an example). In the General Electric/McKinsey matrix the two axes are:

1. Industry attractiveness (which includes the size, growth, diversity, profitability and competitive structure of the industry as well as relevant political, economic, social and technological factors).

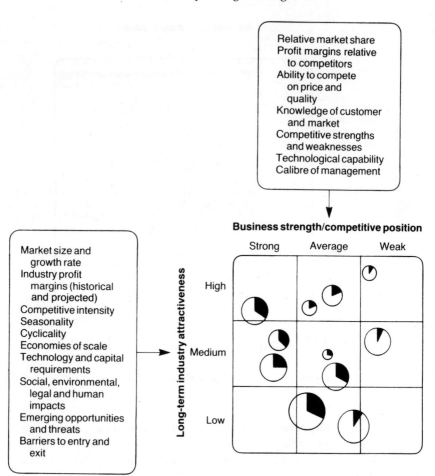

Figure 7.2 General Electric's nine-cell business portfolio matrix.

2. Business strengths (another composite dimension including size, growth, share, position, profitability, image, strengths and weaknesses).

So although this looks to be a more sophisticated model it is far more difficult to plot businesses on the matrix and to interpret what each position means.

Sharing activities: the key to success

In what ways can being part of a corporation benefit an individual business unit? To answer this question we shall use Figure 4.1, the diagram that we developed to analyze strategy at the business level. Figure 7.3 presents one of three basic ways in which connections between business units may be established.

1. *Shared skills and resources.* Here the units benefit from sharing skills and resources. For example, unit X may be particularly good at marketing; unit Y may be in an industry that traditionally has not employed sophisticated marketing strategies. By passing over expertise from unit X, unit Y is able to gain competitive advantages in its industry. Other examples might be the sharing of distribution channels, research facilities, training establishments (see Illustration 7B 'Transferring marketing skills').

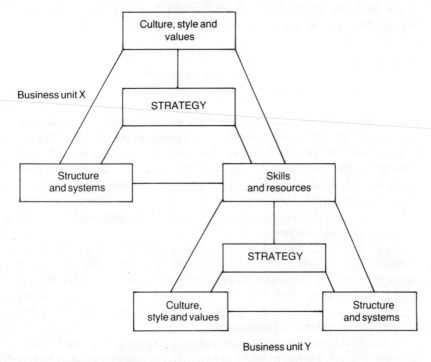

Figure 7.3 Sharing skills and resources.

2. *Sharing structures and systems.* Some conglomerates have added value to their acquisitions by installing better financial and management systems and by reorganizing into divisions of related businesses. In this way sharing of resources and expertise is facilitated.

3. *Sharing culture and values.* Here the individual business unit benefits from the infusion of a common corporate culture and the instilling of a set of core values. For example, if the acquiring corporation has a strong innovative culture, this could rub off on the acquired business to beneficial effect.

Of course, in some circumstances business units will be strengthened by sharing more than one of these three categories, but in practice successful corporations tend to stress one or other of these areas as their route to adding value to the individual businesses. For sharing to be effective the acquired businesses must be in a *related* field, otherwise sharing would either not be feasible or it would not improve the competitive position of the acquired or acquiring business. There is ample evidence that related diversification is better than unrelated (see, for example, M. Porter, *Harvard Business Review*, May–June 1987).

How to diversify?

Our understanding of industry structure would suggest that acquiring an existing firm in the industry might be a better move than starting up a new venture. This is because the start-up business would add capacity to the existing industry, which might increase competition and provoke retaliation. However, there is evidence that internal development might be preferable to acquisition, particularly where the corporation anticipates problems in integrating the acquired firm into its structure and systems.

The problem with acquisitions is that they are likely to have different cultures and shared values. The greater the differences between cultures, the more painful the integration process is likely to be. Thus a long period of in-fighting, conflict and negotiation may ensue following the acquisition, which diverts energy from the improvement of the competitive positions of businesses.

In Japan where, for legal and cultural reasons, acquisitions are difficult, there is a long tradition of firms diversifying through internal development. The start-up venture is spawned by the existing

---

TRANSFERRING MARKETING SKILLS IS HARDER THAN SHIFTING OWNERS

If a company can sell sun oil can it also sell cement?

The trouble with trying to answer this question of transferability is that there are many retailing skills. Making money out of shopkeeping is not just a matter of getting the right products on the counter and selling them with a smile. Merchandising and staff training are important but they are not the only important skills. And some of the most important currently are the most transferable.

Merchandising is pretty specific and specific to individual product areas, not just broad markets. Thus a star wine buyer is important when he helps Tesco win Wine Supermarket of the Year award. But that doesn't mean he could put together a good range of cosmetics.

Operational skills are more easily transferred, although it isn't the same running a small high street shop selling large numbers of small items (like Boots) as running a huge shed selling smaller volumes at larger prices (like Payless).

Even property skills cannot be transferred directly from a high street chain where planning permissions and car parking don't enter the equation to an edge of town operation. And distribution to a smallish chain of stores selling slow-moving goods on the edges of towns demands different techniques from those used to stock the shelves of a large high street chain selling fast moving goods.

But as we head for the 1990s the most successful retailers seem to be those which can harness some of the most easily transferred skills. Technology has helped W.H. Smith, Boots and Marks & Spencer escape the current slaughter in retailing. And personnel skills, especially training, are also important in keeping companies like M & S and Sainsbury in their leading positions.

The DIY stores have hit the headlines with their computerized tills because they manage to charge far too much now and again. But the more legitimate benefits of store computerization lie in telling management what is selling, allowing them to replace items more quickly, to adjust their ranges to reflect what is actually selling and adjust store layout as well, where that seems to make sense. It is curious to think that all those super retailers didn't know what was selling before, but that seems to be the case, and their profits are benefiting enormously now that they do know.

Boots' computers are rated more highly than most in the industry and it looks like they will be walking all over Payless and Halfords before long. But doubts remain about whether the human elements at Boots can apply their skills to DIY as well as their computers.

The Guardian (18 August 1989).

---

corporation; what new skills are required are either developed internally or staff are hired and inculcated into the corporation's ways of doing things. The successful start-ups create a valuable reservoir of organizational experience and confidence; this in turn can create a constructive interdivisional rivalry which spurs others on to succeed with new ventures.

So far we have not mentioned vertical integration as a strategy. This form of diversification moves the firm either forwards into 'downstream' activities (like transport and distribution, or into retailing), or backwards ('upstream') into the control of sources of supply. These moves can be made either through acquisition or through internal development. If the internal development option is chosen, a question that needs to be addressed is whether the firm is capable of effectively carrying out the activity. Although these moves into upstream or downstream activities are related to the firm's original capabilities, in many respects they are moves into new industries.

What makes the clothing manufacturer think he can run a retail chain? Why would the management of a steel mill be any good at running an iron ore mine? Vertical integration is often undertaken to control what are seen as critical activities for the firm's success. We saw in our exploration of organization structure in Chapter 4 that support staff were engaged in activities that could feasibly be subcontracted to an outside supplier. Large machine bureaucracies that are tied to a single industry often opt for vertical integration as a way of controlling as many parts of the operation as possible. Consequently, these types of firm would tend to have well-developed support staffs. Where the activity becomes too large to be controlled effectively under one management structure, or where the vertical integration has been achieved through acquisition, firms tend to opt for a multi-divisional structure. The difference between this form of multi-divisional structure and divisionalized structures found in more diversified corporations is that the vertically integrated corporation must co-ordinate activities closely between the divisions (e.g. the integrated oil company needs to co-ordinate activities right across the exploration, extraction, transportation, refining, distribution and retailing divisions).

When to diversify?

Porter suggests that any potential attempt at diversification should pass three essential tests:

1. *The attractiveness test.* The industries chosen for diversification must be structurally attractive or capable of being made attractive. The problem here is that an attractive industry is likely to be one with high entry barriers (which would deter entry through internal development). Also firms in attractive industries are likely to be expensive to buy. If a firm does appear to be a bargain, the potential purchaser needs to pay close attention to the third test (the 'better-off test'). Structurally unattractive industries should be considered only if there is a possibility of the corporation transforming the economics of the industry through its actions, or if the corporation anticipates an improvement in the industry's structure.

2. *The cost-of-entry test.* Here the golden rule is that the cost of entering the new business must not consume all the future profits. Problems arise where the acquiring corporation finds itself in a bid-battle with a rival. Competitive bidding can lead to the 'lucky' winner paying well over the stock market value of the firm before it came up for sale. There needs to be a great deal of unrealized potential in the acquired business to justify such premium prices.

3. *The better-off test.* The corporation must bring some significant competitive advantage to the new unit, or the new unit must offer potential for significant advantage to the corporation. If that advantage is a one-off restructuring of a sleepy business then the acquiring corporation should sell off the turned-around unit in order to free resources to work the same trick elsewhere. However, some managements confuse shareholder value with size of the corporation and they become reluctant to sell off businesses to which they can no longer add value.

Any move to diversify should produce positive responses to all three questions, not just one or two.

How to structure the corporation?

If there are to be gains from sharing activities between business units then the corporation's structure, systems and culture must facilitate and support the transference of skills and resources. Here are a number of structures and systems that can help the sharing of resources:

1. *Grouping related business units*. This should be done on the basis of those interrelationships between businesses that are most critical to achieving competitive advantage. Potential benefits might accrue from relationships based on related production systems, access to common customers or sharing R&D expertise.

2. *Partial centralization*. Here certain activities are carried out centrally which benefit all business units (e.g. purchasing, order processing, distribution).

3. *Committees and taskforces*. These are simply devices to get people to talk to each other on a regular basis. One of the reasons that claims about the benefits of synergy were never realized is that too little thought and effort was put into encouraging communication across businesses.

4. *Horizontal incentives*. Most management incentives are based on business unit performance, thus co-operation and sharing may well be actively discouraged through the reward system. There should be some positive encouragement for executives to co-operate with other business units (e.g. a proportion of the bonus based on group performance).

5. *Rotate managers between business units*. In this way managers get to see directly how and where co-operation and sharing can benefit the business unit. It also helps to set up useful information networks across units and can enhance feelings of belonging to a corporate 'whole', not just an autonomous business unit.

Some corporations have achieved co-ordination across business units by intervening directly in the strategic planning processes of the individual business unit. This strategic planning style is just one of a number of different approaches to managing corporations identified by Goold and Campbell. They investigated a number of large, multi-business corporations with a view to determining what struc-

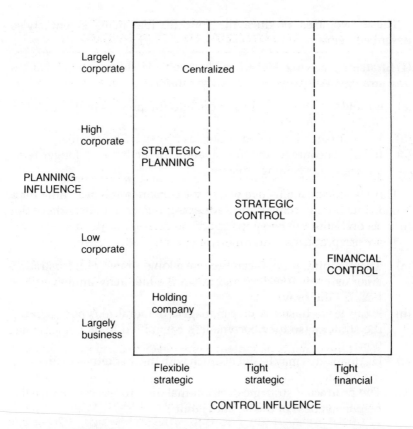

Figure 7.4 Strategic management styles. (Adapted from M. Goold and A. Campbell, *Strategies and Styles* (Oxford: Basil Blackwell, 1987).)

tures and corporate management styles were most effective. Their conclusions support a contingency approach to corporate management style; there is no one best way, it all depends on the situation.

In Figure 7.4 the two axes are planning influence and control influence. Where planning influence is high the headquarters of the corporation takes a leading role in determining business unit strategy; where it is low each business unit is left, more or less, to sort out its own strategy. Control influence refers to the setting of tough profit targets and budgets centrally. Clear short-term targets are set, performance is carefully monitored, and business unit managers are held to account for variances from the budgets.

127

These two axes produce the four feasible management styles described below.

(1) Strategic planning. HQ is heavily involved in formulating business unit strategy. Advantages of this style include:

(a) It builds in checks and balances into the process of determining business unit strategy.
(b) It encourages integrated strategies across business units.
(c) It can encourage the formulation of ambitious, longer-term strategies for gaining advantage.

This style is most effective where the corporation is searching for a broad, integrated strategy for developing business units, where the focus is on long-term competitive advantage.

There are problems with this style:

(a) The planning process can become a long, drawn out, frustrating affair as plans travel up and down the hierarchy until everyone has had their say.
(b) It can leave business unit managers demoralized, not 'owning' the strategy (so they become less committed to its implementation).
(c) HQ managers may be out of touch with the marketplace served by the business unit.
(d) The protracted strategic decision-making process can reduce the responsiveness of the business unit.

(2) Financial control. This is the reverse of the strategic planning style. Here the business unit managers make their own strategy but they have to meet centrally determined budgets. The advantages of this approach include:

(a) It strongly motivates managers to improve short-term performance.
(b) It forces managers to address weaknesses in existing strategies.
(c) It can encourage the development of managers who, with this style, are given profit responsibility at early stages in their careers.
(d) This style is particularly useful in conglomerates, where HQ management does not have the intimate knowledge of each business's industry and markets.

This style does not encourage sharing of activities and skills, and its excessively short-term orientation can be disastrous in industries which require a longer-term perspective on investment decisions.

Lastly, the rigid adherence to budgets (which seems to be an inevitable feature of this style) can lead to lost opportunities and demoralized managers.

(3) Strategic control. Companies that opt for this style aim to get all the benefits of the first two styles without their attendant disadvantages. Not surprisingly, therefore, this style is the most difficult to apply. Plans are made at the business unit level but are closely scrutinized at HQ. Financial targets are set centrally, which may lead to the plan and the budget pulling in different directions (e.g. medium- and long-term investment programs conflicting with short-term profit targets). Corporations using this style may adhere to the Boston matrix form of portfolio management. If they do, the managers of the cash cows may feel aggrieved at not being viewed as a growth prospect. (How would you feel if your business was classified as a dog?)

The main disadvantage with this style is that the strategic and financial objectives, the long- and short-term goals make accountability less clear-cut and create ambiguity. Managers at the business unit level can be uncertain about whether they are supposed to put forward aggressive long-term growth plans, or plans which deliver tight adherence to shorter-term performance targets.

(4) Holding company style. In organizations that adopt this style, the HQ makes little effort to influence business units. Goold and Campbell's research led them to conclude that successful companies who started out with this approach, soon moved to one of the other three styles.

The way in which the centre (or HQ) of a diversified company controls subsidiaries can determine the extent to which value is added to each business. Goold and Campbell suggest that appropriate corporate controls can assist the subsidiary in several ways. The control process can encourage greater clarity and realism in the planning process. The need to satisfy a critical HQ audience helps to ensure that managers of subsidiaries produce robust plans, particularly in the details of implementation. Secondly, the corporate control process tends to encourage more objectivity in the formulation of plans, forcing managers to justify their preferences.

The corporate HQ that sets demanding goals for subsidiaries is likely to promote improved performance. In contrast, the management team of a firm facing a weak shareholder grouping is less likely to set itself challenging goals. However, judging whether or not a goal is stretching management is difficult, especially where the corporate HQ is not particularly knowledgeable about the conditions in the subsidiary's industry. If unrealistic goals are set this will tend to demotivate rather than motivate management.

Where the corporation keeps a close eye on subsidiaries then it is able to make the necessary interventions should the business run into problems. Timing of these interventions is considerably assisted where clear targets (or 'milestones') have been built into the control process. Where the centre operates poor strategic control processes, not only might these benefits of strategic control not accrue, the corporation may actually subtract value from the business units (making the corporation a prime target for 'unbundling'). Objectives that are too rigid, that emphasize measurable rather than appropriate outcomes, and untimely and meddlesome interference from HQ, can combine to demoralize the subsidiary management and encourage the implementation of the wrong strategies.

Global strategy

There are basically two types of international industry:

1. *Multi-domestic industry*. In this type of industry structure international business is really just a collection of domestic industries. Competitive advantage in one country is more or less independent of competition in others.
2. *Global industry*. In global industries competitive advantage in one country is strongly influenced by position in others. Global industry rivals are pitted against each other worldwide.

In some industries many of the activities involved in production, marketing and servicing need to be tailored to the particular requirements of the country. Here tailoring is critical to competitive advantage. These types of industry would therefore tend to be multi-domestic in structure.

Other industries do not need to be so country specific. In these industries advantage can be gained through operating and organizing on a global basis:

1. *Economies of scale*. By offering standard products across many markets the benefits of large-scale operations can be achieved.

2. *Experience curve advantages*. Firms can benefit from sharing resources and experiences across countries.

3. *Advantages from location*. It may be cheaper to produce components in one country, assemble them in another, and it may be more effective to locate fundamental R&D in a third country. The global company can pick the most advantageous locations for different parts of the business.

4. *Differentiate with multinational buyers*. If your customers are multinationals, it may pay for you to organize on a global scale to service them (e.g. consider the trend for accountancy practices to go global to service better their multinational clients; also most of the large engineering contractors are organized globally to serve, in part, their global customers).

These and other advantages may accrue if a firm organizes on a global basis. However, many corporations have experienced great difficulty in reaping the rewards of 'going global'. Rather like some of the barriers to sharing in the diversified corporation, global companies have difficulty in getting subsidiaries in different countries to co-operate with each other. Quite understandably, the management team in the country subsidiary wants to control as much of the business as it can: after all, they will be held accountable for its performance. This makes them reluctant to buy-in components, finished products, design, R&D, etc. from other group companies.

The challenge facing the global company is how to respond to the particular needs of individual countries whilst at the same time not jeopardizing the advantages of being part of a global company. There are a few branded products that are marketed in the same way across the globe (e.g. Coca-Cola, Marlboro), but these tend to be exceptions. Most global corporations adapt either the products or the marketing approach to the particular requirements of each country. For example, Schweppes tonic water is advertised as a mixer for alcoholic drinks in the UK but as a soft drink in France. Timotei, Unilever's global shampoo brand, is promoted with the same healthy image worldwide, but the product is changed to suit the varying ways that different nationalities wash their hair.

Managers, then, need to be encouraged to seek out the benefits that can be gained through global co-operation. A gradual process can help to build confidence in moving the country managers from a wholly country orientation to more of a global orientation. This can start with the sharing of information, then seminars, conferences and exchanges

131

of personnel can be organized to encourage the establishment of personal networks and a feeling of being part of a global company. Then tangible projects can be set up to see, for instance, what benefits could accrue from organizing purchasing on a regional (or even global) scale. These tentative steps can be reinforced through adjustments to the managers' incentive systems. The ultimate expression of the global company is the reconfiguration of the entire organization along global lines. This is the place to end, not begin, a move to globalization.

In a major study of international competitiveness Michael Porter concludes that in order for a country's industry to be successful in global markets it needs to have:

1. *Favourable factor conditions*. These include the availability of key resources (including skills, infrastructure and research institutes). His study also found that, where countries had selective factor *disadvantages* they were forced to innovate to overcome (or work around) these problems. This, in turn, has formed the basis of competitive advantage (e.g. if a nation experiences high energy costs early this forces the need to develop energy-efficient products and processes which are subsequently demanded worldwide).

2. *Demand conditions*. There must be a strong home demand for sophisticated products. Compliant domestic consumers are a disadvantage as they do not pressure the industry into innovation and excellence.

3. *Relating and supporting industries*. A network of supporting and related industries seems to help industries achieve global superiority. For example, Sweden's leading position in pulp and paper is supported by a network of related industries (packaging, chemicals, wood-processing machinery, conveyor systems, boilers, drying machinery, speciality truck manufacture). In many of these supporting industries these Swedish firms have achieved leading positions globally too.

4. *Firm strategy, structure and rivalry*. Perhaps the most important of these factors is the extent of rivalry in the domestic industry. The evidence strongly supports the view that domestic competition is vital. Conversely, where governments have encouraged mergers to create national monopolies (to get the 'critical mass' required to be a global player) these monopolies have not, on the whole, been successful in establishing a global position. Bitter rivalry between

local firms has acted as the spur to innovate. There are no excuses in a competitive rivalry between domestic firms: they both play on the same playing-field. It appears that any sacrifice of economies of scale that may result from amalgamating domestic firms is more than offset by the benefits of keen rivalry.

Appendix:
Workgear case analysis

Introduction

This analysis results from a large number of case study sessions held with managers from a wide variety of organizations. It does not purport to be an answer: there is never just one solution to the problems facing a firm. However, it does show how a structured approach to analysis can help in unravelling the key strategic issues facing an organization.

The analysis has been subdivided into five sections. Each section relates to the questions set at the end of Chapters 2–6.

Chapter two

We can use the information in the case study to make some useful inferences about the nature of the industry that Workgear is in. But defining the industry poses some problems.

If you have tried to apply the Five Forces model to the case you may have found that there are some contradictory factors influencing the strength of some of the five forces. For instance, there is evidence that Workgear face powerful buyers (the linen hire company that took the best six quotations and divided the order among them at the price given in the lowest quote). On the other hand, some final user firms (like BAA) are relatively inexperienced in purchasing from this industry and are more likely to be looking for a longer-term relationship with a supplier.

One way to resolve the problem is to conduct a five forces analysis for the two main customer groups served by Workgear: the linen hire companies and the final user buyers.

Linen hire

Intensity of rivalry

1. Intense competition based on price.
2. Many firms in the industry, all seem to be of similar size, and capability.
3. No clear evidence of growing demand.
4. Switching costs of buyers are low to non-existent.
5. The product (standard workwear) is more or less a commodity.

Threat of entry

Although there is intense rivalry in this industry (and you may conclude that firms might not wish to enter it) this competitive force is about what barriers to entry there might be, whether or not firms want to enter the industry. We need to bear in mind that the structure of the industry might change – some marginal firms might leave the industry, demand might expand – making entry a more attractive proposition.

1. There do not appear to be any significant economies of scale in this industry.
2. There would be some cost benefits to be had from accumulating experience in clothing manufacture. This might mean that a manufacturer of clothing (e.g. jeans) could put in a speculative tender for a linen hire contract (if the firm had spare capacity, for instance). This firm might be able to price very competitively (marginal cost plus some contribution to overheads).
3. There is no evidence of brand loyalty: linen hire firms seem to buy on price.
4. Distribution channels and capital costs are not significant entry barriers.

Threat of substitutes

Linen hire buyers purchase workwear from this industry so that they can provide a service to their customers. What other options do they have, apart from buying from Workgear's industry? They could purchase disposable clothing (if this was viable and feasible). Depending on how broadly we define Workgear's industry, the linen hire firms could purchase from outside this industry (e.g. imports from South-east Asia or Eastern Europe).

Power of buyers

1. The linen hire customers are few in number (two or three) and they purchase large quantities from each supplying firm.
2. As clothing forms a significant component of a linen hire firm's costs, they are likely to pursue vigorously ways of cutting these costs.
3. Workgear's industry is populated by large numbers of small suppliers.
4. Linen hire buyers incur very low switching costs.
5. The linen hire buyers are very knowledgeable about Workgear's industry (they can tell Workgear how much it costs to make a garment).

Power of suppliers

1. Workgear purchases cloth from one supplier. We do not know whether there is an alternative source of this type of cloth, nor do we know whether Klopmans are exploiting Workgear's apparent dependence on them. We also know little about where other firms in the industry obtain their cloth supplies.
2. Workgear uses relatively unskilled labour (and trains them in a fairly short space of time). It does not appear that the supply of this type of labour is a significant problem at the moment.
3. The industry uses conventional machinery which is unlikely to be in restricted supply.

Summary of the linen hire industry segment

There would seem to be three strong forces at work in the linen hire segment. Buyers are very powerful, rivalry is intense and entry looks relatively easy. There would not appear to be strong threats from substitutes at present; the cloth suppliers Klopmans could exploit Workgear's short-term dependence on them.

Final user

Intensity of rivalry

1. Compared with the linen hire segment, there would appear to be fewer firms currently operating in the final user segment.

2. Competition in this segment is likely to be less intense than in linen hire, partly because the buyers are purchasing not just on price (e.g. they are interested in other, more qualitative product attributes, like design flair, flexibility, a good working relationship, variety).

3. Demand is likely to be growing in this segment as more firms see the benefits of 'tailor made' workwear.

4. Firms, like Workgear, have an opportunity to build a reputation in the industry, and buyers are likely to incur significant switching costs (tangible costs like needing to explain to a new supplier their requirements; and intangible switching costs like loyalty to their existing suppliers, feelings of comfort and familiarity with them).

Threat of entry
Compared with the linen hire segment, it would seem to be more difficult to get into the final user segment:

1. Existing final user buyers demonstrate some loyalty. Reputation seems to count.

2. Additional skills are required (in design, sales and service).

Threat of substitutes
Here we need to ask what needs are being met when the final user customers buy workwear from this industry. In addition to the basic requirements of keeping your workforce clean, and conforming to health and safety legislation (needs which also apply to the linen hire segment), the final user buyers are purchasing for other reasons:

1. To promote a corporate image or identity.

2. To motivate staff and build a team spirit.

If we take the corporate identity need first, this need can be met in many different ways:

1. Corporate advertising.

2. Redesigning the logo.
3. Sponsoring a golf tournament.

Similarly, the motivational and morale-boosting needs can be met through:

1. Management and supervisor training.
2. Team-building activities.
3. Pay and other perks.
4. Singing company songs.

So the final user buyers may be attracted to quite diverse substitute suppliers if Workgear's industry became complacent or expensive.

Power of buyers

1. Final user buyers are many, and they are not organized.
2. Final user buyers are fairly ignorant of Workgear's industry.
3. The clothing items bought are not likely to form a significant cost element.
4. Final user buyers have significant switching costs and are likely to display loyalty to a single supplier.

Power of suppliers
Compared with the supplies needed to serve the linen hire customers, there is some good news and some bad. Due to the diverse requirements of final user customers, Workgear and its competitors should be able to shop around and use different suppliers for different fabrics. On the downside, design talent is required, which may be in short supply.

Summary of final user segment
Intensity of rivalry and power of buyers are significantly lower in this segment. Buyers are likely to be less price sensitive than linen hire buyers. Entry also looks more difficult. On the other hand, there is a stronger threat from substitutes, and there may be a problem with the supply of some skills.

On balance the final user segment is structurally more attractive than the linen hire segment.

PEST analysis and competitor analysis

There is not enough information in the case to enable us to get very far with these two additional analyses.

Chapter three

Linen hire buyers' needs

1. Bulk orders.
2. Standard products to a tight specification, durable cloth.
3. Low prices.
4. Limited variety.
5. Guaranteed delivery (though not urgent delivery).

Final user buyers' needs

1. Customization.
2. Flexibility.
3. Short runs.
4. Design assistance, ability to interpret customer needs.
5. High quality: fabrics, fashion, fit.
6. After-sales support, replacement service.
7. Prompt delivery.

Appropriate generic strategies

To serve the linen hire buyers effectively a strategy of cost leadership would be appropriate, producing standard, no-frills (literally) garments, and driving costs down as low as possible. If the firm chose to serve only linen hire customers (and if the firm dedicated its operations to meet these buyers' needs), then the strategy would be focused cost leadership strategy.

If we assume that the final users are prepared to pay a premium price (if you can meet their requirements), then a differentiation strategy would be appropriate. The scope of the strategy (broad or narrow) would depend on whether Workgear sought to serve all types of final user customer, or to concentrate on a subsegment (e.g. high-tech firms or airlines).

Chapter four

What would Workgear look life if it were to serve:

1. Just the linen hire segment?
2. Just the final user segment?
3. Both segments?

Linen hire: ideal organization

Skills and resources
1. Buying.
2. Pool of low-cost labour.
3. Large batch production system: factory space, efficient machinery.
4. Production management expertise.
5. Supervisory skills.
6. Work study skills.

Structure and systems
1. High specialization in operating core: routine work.
2. Clear hierarchy and reporting relationships.
3. Well-defined jobs.
4. Technostructure staff: work study, production scheduling and control, quality assurance.
5. Management information system to monitor and control costs across the whole organization.
6. Systems for: stock control, work-in-progress control, training, maintenance.
7. Incentive systems.

Culture, style and values
1. Efficiency and cost control values pervade the organization.
2. Strong, centralized management style.
3. Bureaucratic (in its best sense) culture.

Final user: ideal organization

Skills and resources
1. Design (specifically, the ability to interpret customer needs and to translate them into manufacturable and profitable products).
2. Sales and marketing skills (to secure the business).
3. After-sales service.
4. Flexible, skilled operatives (to cope with changing patterns, cloths etc.).
5. Purchasing skills.
6. Reliable distribution.
7. Computer-aided design, and computer-aided manufacturing (to enable customers to see various designs, colours; direct links between design and cloth-cutting machinery).

Structure and systems
1. Flexible structure, short hierarchy to facilitate vertical and horizontal communication.
2. Sales/design/procurement/production/distribution must be well co-ordinated.
3. Individuals responsible for liaising with customers and progressing their orders.
4. Good estimating and costing systems.
5. Quality assurance systems.

Culture, style and values
1. Entrepreneurial, but 'professional' culture that values individual contributions and initiatives.
2. 'Customer service' as a strong shared value.
3. Good relationships between departments, and between management and shopfloor.
4. Consultative management styles.

Figures A.1 and A.2 use the value chain to depict the main requirements of the two segments.

Serving both segments: ideal organization

If we compare the different organizational requirements that derive from serving these two segments we can judge the extent to which it is feasible for a firm to serve both segments simultaneously. There are some requirements that are shared by both segments, for example:

1. Procurement skills.
2. Quality assurance systems.
3. Cost-monitoring and control systems.

There are other requirements that are similar, but there is a different emphasis required for each segment. For example, if we take the need for production scheduling and control systems, we find that the linen hire requirement is for a system that can cope with large batches of standard items. Whereas a different kind of system would be needed to cope with the small batches of very variable products that are required to meet the needs of final user buyers.

There are other organizational requirements that vary substantially between the two segments:

1. Organization structure (well defined, hierarchical for linen hire; looser, flexible, short hierarchy for final user).
2. Values (efficiency, cost control versus customer service).
3. Styles (centralized, autocratic versus consultative).
4. Culture (bureaucratic versus entrepreneurial).

These differences may well be important to the firm's ability to deliver above-average performance in these two segments. The extent to which a firm compromises between these differing requirements will therefore affect its ability to outperform its rivals, especially those firms that have opted to focus exclusively on one or other of these segments.

This analysis also gives us some clues about how a firm might organize to minimize the compromises inherent in this dual strategy. Some activities could be shared without detriment to performance. But it would appear that the different structures, styles and cultures would

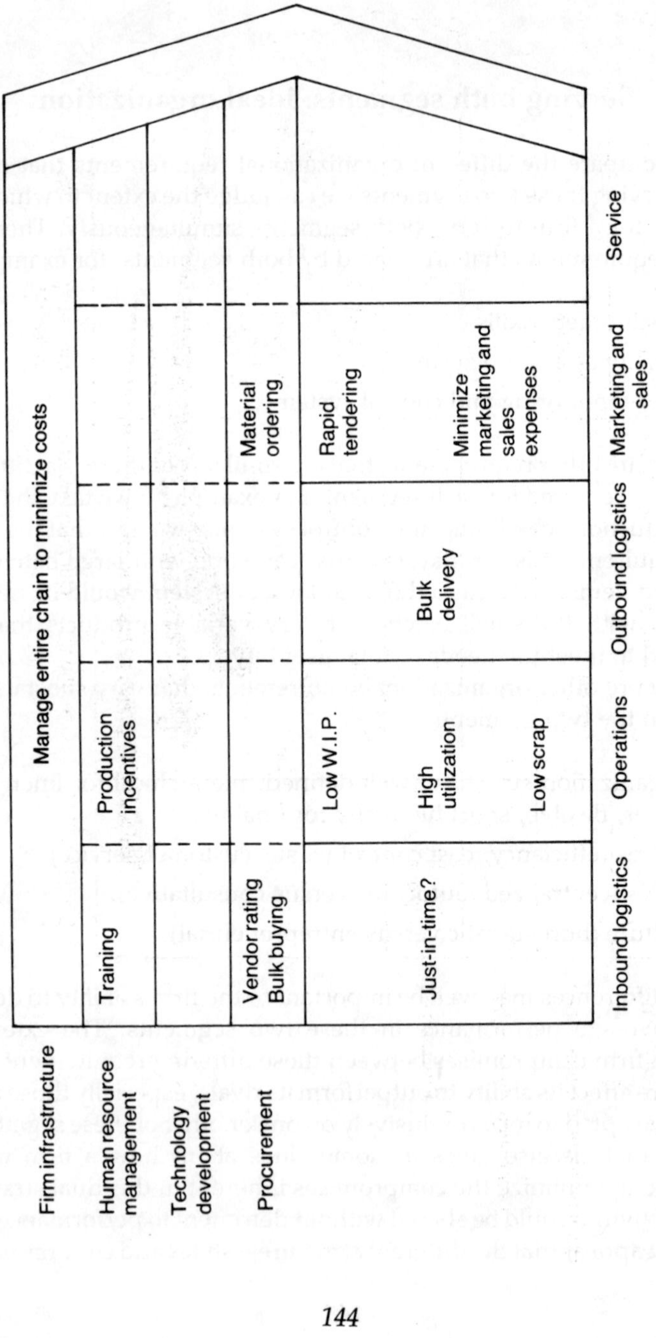

Figure A.1 Linen hire segment.

Firm infrastructure	Manage entire chain to minimize costs				
Human resource management	Training	Production incentives			
Technology development					
Procurement	Vendor rating Bulk buying		Material ordering		
	Just-in-time?	Low W.I.P.		Rapid tendering	
		High utilization	Bulk delivery	Minimize marketing and sales expenses	
		Low scrap			
	Inbound logistics	Operations	Outbound logistics	Marketing and sales	Service

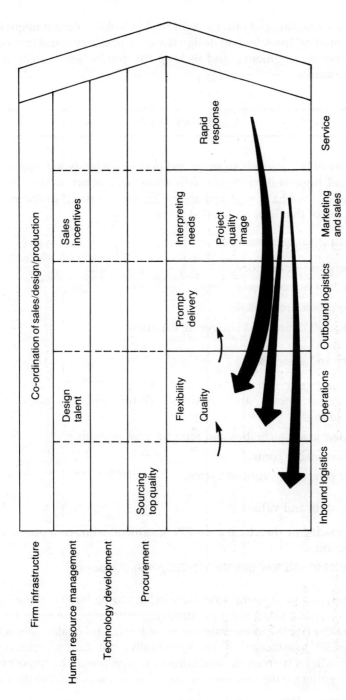

Figure A.2 Final user segment.

argue for separating out other activities. A possible solution might be to 'divisionalize' the sales and design teams so that they could focus on their respective segments, and to keep the production system as a shared resource.

Chapter five

The reality of Workgear is summarized in the case study in Chapter 1. The actual organization clearly falls some way short of the 'ideal' organizations we have explored above. There are critical problems in many areas of the firm, as detailed below.

Skills and resources

1. Poorly laid-out factory.
2. A lack of management talent.
3. Poor procurement skills.
4. A lack of costing and budgeting expertise.

Structure and systems

1. An emergent structure which is ambiguous (Is Stan Lewis in charge or not?) and muddled (Why separate sales and marketing?).
2. Unclear responsibilities and reporting relationships.
3. *Ad hoc* quality control.
4. Poor production control systems.

Culture, style and values

1. The managing director is a meddling autocrat who is not providing direction.
2. Suspicion and low morale in management group.

On the positive side the workforce seems to be happy, there has been some recent investment in improving efficiency, the order book looks healthy (for the immediate future, at least), and quality seems to be generally satisfactory. More specifically, the firm's reputation coupled with its (perceived) strengths in design would be important factors in going for the final user market. But we cannot ignore the fact that profitability has been declining steadily despite increases in sales, and there are major problems with the management structure.

Comparing the ideal organization with the actual organization should give us some idea of the extent of change required to transform the firm. Here you need to exercise judgement, and rather than try to work through the three strategic options (linen hire, final user, or both) select one and complete the chart in Figure 5.2.

Chapter six

Let us assume that Workgear has decided to target the final user segment and to phase out its linen hire business (as a result of the industry analysis). Using the force field analysis we might identify the following pushing and resisting forces:

1. Pushing forces:
   (a) Les Barnes is worried.
   (b) Some design talent already in the firm.
   (c) A good reputation.
   (d) A happy workforce.
   (e) The drive and ideas of Stan Lewis.

2. Resisting forces
   (a) Demoralized management.
   (b) Complacent workforce.
   (c) Autocratic styles.
   (d) Les Barnes.
   (e) Communication problems between management.

These are just some examples, not an exhaustive list.

Can any of these forces be strengthened? Perhaps someone (like Stan Lewis) can work on Les Barnes's vague feelings of unease to galvanize him into taking some initiatives (like stepping down). Stan could provide the leadership and direction required if he was given his head and entrusted with steering the firm towards the new strategy.

New pushing forces could come from outside (the bank, recruit new management), and some actions could serve to both strengthen pushing forces and reduce resisting forces (like a drive to gear up the quality systems).

With regard to priorities, nothing will happen until the management team is sorted out. Barnes must step aside (he is probably not able to change, and he is close to retirement). Either promote Stan Lewis or bring someone in from outside (in which case Stan would probably leave). Then a clear vision about where the firm is heading needs to be communicated to all the staff.

Recommended reading

There are two good general strategic management textbooks available in the UK:

Cliff Bowman and David Asch, *Strategic Management* (Basingstoke: Macmillan, 1987). This contains a separate chapter on strategy in not-for-profit organizations.

Gerry Johnson and Kevan Scholes, *Exploring Corporate Strategy: Text and cases* (Hemel Hempstead: Prentice Hall International, 1988).

Michael Porter's two influential contributions are: *Competitive Strategy* (New York: Free Press, 1980) and *Competitive Advantage* (New York: Free Press, 1985). These are both large texts, and although well written can be rather heavy going. However, you may find that the examples and checklists that Porter develops useful in relating his ideas to your firm's situation.

The latest in the 'Excellence' series is Tom Peters's *Thriving on Chaos* (Basingstoke: Macmillan, 1987). If you have not read any of the other books by Peters and Waterman, you would do just as well to start with this one.

Index

151

Index